BRIGHT NOTES

WALDEN AND ON THE DUTY OF CIVIL DISOBEDIENCE
BY
HENRY DAVID THOREAU

Intelligent Education

Nashville, Tennessee

BRIGHT NOTES: Walden and On the Duty of Civil Disobedience by Henry David Thoreau

www.BrightNotes.com

No part of this publication may be used or reproduced in any manner whatsoever without written permission, except in the case of brief quotations in critical articles and reviews. For permissions, contact Influence Publishers http://www.influencepublishers.com.

ISBN: 978-1-645421-86-3 (Paperback)
ISBN: 978-1-645421-87-0 (eBook)

Published in accordance with the U.S. Copyright Office Orphan Works and Mass Digitization report of the register of copyrights, June 2015.

Originally published by Monarch Press.
Charlotte A. Alexander, 1965
2020 Edition published by Influence Publishers.

Interior design by Lapiz Digital Services. Cover Design by Thinkpen Designs.

Printed in the United States of America.

Library of Congress Cataloging-in-Publication Data forthcoming.
Names: Intelligent Education
Title: BRIGHT NOTES: Walden and On the Duty of Civil Disobedience by Henry David Thoreau
Subject: STU004000 STUDY AIDS / Book Notes

CONTENTS

1) Introduction To Henry David Thoreau — 1

2) Detailed Summary: Walden — 11

3) Walden: Textual Analysis — 25
    Chapters 5 – 8 — 25
    Chapters 9 – 18 — 38

4) On The Duty Of Civil Disobedience — 54

5) Selected Poems — 59

6) Critical Commentary — 63

7) Essay Questions And Answers — 75

8) Bibliography And Guide To Research Papers — 80

INTRODUCTION TO HENRY DAVID THOREAU

Henry David Thoreau was born in Concord, Massachusetts, on July 12, 1817. After graduating from Harvard in 1837, he taught school, first at Concord, then in a private school opened with his brother John. He also began keeping his Journal upon graduation, and in 1837 made Emerson's acquaintance. During the period after college he began giving lectures and publishing essays, chiefly in the *Week* and the *Dial* (a Transcendental journal). He lived with the Emersons in 1841, and again after the Walden experience (1845-47), supervising the household in Emerson's frequent absence. From 1844 onward, making a living also included for him brief periods in his father's pencil-making factory and surveying. Also, from 1839 he was periodically making excursions on the Concord and Merrimack rivers and into the Maine woods and Cape Cod, the basis of later published writings. He went to Minnesota for his health in 1861, and died at Concord of tuberculosis on May 6, 1862.

BIOGRAPHICAL HIGHLIGHTS OF THOREAU'S LIFE

From the brief biographical summary above emerge certain areas of some significance to the reader to Thoreau's work: the period right after college, including what appear to have been the two loves in his life, and his unending conflict about choosing a profession; his friendship with Ralph Waldo Emerson and his interest in Transcendentalism; and of course the excursions into "Nature" which produced his major works. It is generally assumed that he loved (but did not marry) two women in his life: one was Ellen Sewall, sister of his friend Edmund Sewall, to whom he proposed in the years after college and was rejected; the other was Lidian Emerson, wife of Ralph Waldo Emerson, a woman beautiful and severe, 15 years his senior, to whom he seems to have been devoted platonically for a number of years. Just out of college Thoreau was plagued with both choosing a profession suitable for a Harvard graduate, and with simply earning a living. Although he never found himself able to fit into any of the categories assumed suitable for his education- divinity, law, academic teaching, lecturing and research - and throughout his life elevated (as had Emerson in "The American Scholar") the "poet-philosopher" as his own ideal, he was annoyingly confronted from time to time with the problem of making a living: hence his periodic teaching and lecturing, his stays with the Emersons during which time he was supposed to "make it" in the New York literary world (but did not), his frustrated periods of work in his father's pencil-making factory, surveying, and the day-labor he did while at Walden and on other excursions. Thoreau's strong resistance to the drudgery necessary to make a go of it in the material world was of course linked to his belief that man should pursue his higher nature, discover his inner self, probably through isolated meditation in a time of leisure; when forced into the hustling economic world he felt his life to be "prosaic, hard and coarse." In an essay "Life Without Principle," for example, he expressed his bitterness by asserting, "a man had better starve at once than lose his innocence in the process of getting his bread."

The influence of his Transcendentalist mentor Emerson upon Thoreau was of course great, both through Emerson's writings such as "The American Scholar" (in which he idealizes the scholar's life of meditation and study) and "Nature" (in which we find the seed of many of Thoreau's ideas about Nature and man), and through his friendship with the Emersons. Yet their friendship proved a difficult one in which Thoreau seems to have invoked an impossible ideal of communication on a "higher plane" between two philosophers. If Thoreau was idealistic, Emerson himself may have been slightly patronizing to the younger man: the inevitable result at any rate was antagonism, expressed for example in an excerpt from Thoreau's Journal - "Talked, or tried to talk, with R.W.E. Lost my time - nay, almost my identity. He, assuming a false opposition where there was no difference of opinion, talked to the wind - told me what I knew - and I lost my time trying to imagine myself somebody else to oppose him." His first stay with the Emersons, however (and tutoring Emerson's nephew on Staten Island), solidified his desires to withdraw from the civilized world for awhile; he wrote in the Journal, "I don't want to feel as if my life were a sojourn any longer. The philosophy cannot be true which so paints it. It is time now that I begin to live." Hence the Walden experiment.

Friendship to Thoreau, though, was the highest Transcendental relation, without which Nature was not morally significant. Thus he went to Emerson (whose essay "Nature" had become the bible of the Transcendentalists) hoping that their relationship would be so ideal as to show the world "what men can build each other up to be, when both master and pupil work in love." [Basically, Transcendentalism explores the nature of reality, and there are several "philosophies" which fall into the general category of Transcendentalism; here we are concerned with an American Transcendentalism propounded chiefly in the ideas of Emerson, based on the search for reality through spiritual intuition.] Thoreau was able to respond intellectually to Emerson, however, in the sense that his own Transcendentalist ideas developed from those set forth in Emerson's famous essay "Nature." Briefly, those ideas, basic to the American Transcendentalist movement, are 1) conviction of knowledge beyond that given to us through the five senses; 2) spirit is supreme over matter; 3) Nature is to be enjoyed, even reverenced; 4) the individual must set a high standard of personal conduct, which often includes an anti-materialistic view of the business world.

THOREAU'S WORKS

Thoreau's chief works are *A Week on the Concord and Merrimack Rivers* (1849), *Walden* (1854), *The Maine Woods* (1863), certain essays such as "On the Duty of Civil Disobedience" (1849), "Slavery in Massachusetts" (1854), and "A Plea for John Brown" (1859). In addition there are now published his Journal accounts of various excursions, and letters and poems, all of which can be found in the standard edition of his works, *The Writings of Henry David Thoreau* (Boston, 1906, 20 volumes). (Many of his essays, in other words, were first presented as lectures or published in journals such as *Dial* and *The Atlantic Monthly*, and were in fact only collected posthumously.) A comment can be added here about *A Week on the Concord and Merrimack Rivers*, published in 1849, two years after Thoreau emerged from Walden Woods; for he wrote this series of essays while at Walden, and it can be said to encompass his spiritual history from 1839 to 1849 (just as *Walden* spans the spiritual struggles of 1845 to 1854). These two may be regarded as companion volumes, chronicling his search for an organic life in Nature, from the easy, youthful communions to the intellectually harder-won communions of his adulthood. He himself financed the publication of the book, and was disappointed in its lack of popular success. Just like *Walden*, *A Week* [it is often referred to as *Week* by biographers and critics] reveals as much of the poet-philosopher as it does of the traveler-sojourner.

THOREAU'S MAJOR THEMES AND IDEAS: SELF-AWARENESS

Thoreau's essential **theme** is life-but life lived when one is fully awake. As a Transcendentalist he was bound to explore the meaning of reality and seek his own inner self. This is why such a volume as *Walden* is both an experience lived and an experience reflected upon: while at Walden from 1845-57 he of course kept his daily journal, but the book he published was the outgrowth of reflections upon that past experiment and experience. *Walden* chronicles the spiritual self-searching of 1845 to 1854, which very importantly includes Thoreau's struggle to recapture afterwards the purity and union with Nature that he felt in his simplified physical existence at Walden Pond. He did not look upon his withdrawal to Walden in the search for self-realization, incidentally, as a permanently desirable isolation from society; but, as one of his critics, Sherman Paul, puts it, "self-realization in Nature suffused him with love. Neither life nor love could be shared, he learned, until he had found his own center, the pride that rested on the security of his own self-reliance."

To find that center of the self, however, Thoreau believed that a "doctrine of simplicity" was desirable; the physically simplified life was the best means to self-emancipation. Through a kind of voluntary poverty, a materially simple existence, a direct line of communication between the inner self and Nature might be established. Thus he chose the pastoral life as the ideal milieu. In his Journal he wrote, "There are two kinds of simplicity, one that is akin to foolishness, the other to wisdom. The philosopher's style of living is only outwardly simple, but inwardly complex. The savage's style is both outwardly and inwardly simple." Thoreau is not, then, merely glorifying the life of the savage in his doctrine of simplicity (some of the American Transcendentalists, along with their counterparts among the English Romantic poets such as William Wordsworth and Samuel Taylor Coleridge, had elevated the primitive life as such, a tendency usually referred to as primitivism); a pastoral life is not necessarily a primitive life, as Thoreau was aware from his days at the pond and in Concord pastures when contrasted to life in the wilder Maine woods. Nor did he view the withdrawal to pastoral life at Walden Pond as escape but rather as discovery and strengthening of his higher nature which he might then bring back into communion with society.

NATURE VS. "BARBARIC" CIVILIZATION

It is true, however, that the idealization of Nature was typical both of Transcendental thought in general and of Thoreau's personal philosophy. Nature administered to both physical and spiritual needs; there was a "correspondence" between man and Nature - that is, every fact of Nature corresponded ideally with a fact of consciousness in man's mind. Or, to put it another way, everything in Nature could be taken possession of by the human mind. Furthermore, experience in Nature became later idealized, "folded many times thick," as Thoreau described his experience at Walden as it had matured through his Journal into the final version. Thoreau also described this correspondence between man and Nature in a poem titled "The Inward Morning":

Packed in my mind lie all the clothes Which outward nature wears, And in its fashion's hourly change It all things else repairs.

In vain I look for change abroad, And can no difference find, Till some new ray of peace uncalled Illumes my inmost mind.

This inward morning is the kind of wakeful awareness he stresses throughout Walden, for example; it assesses the constant inspiration to be derived from Nature. What he was ultimately aiming at of course, as philosopher and Transcendentalist, was union or a sense of complete oneness with Nature: in order to achieve this he attempted a disciplined, ascetic life - the idea of purity, purification of the channels of perception, often recurs in his writing - and he observes Nature closely, practically gives himself up to the life in Nature.

It is only natural that such a philosophy should emerge as anti-materialistic; added to this was Thoreau's personal distaste for materialistic striving, his refusal to subscribe to the prevailing Puritan work ethic, his dislike of organized authority (of church or state, for instance), and his disgust with the way civilized society seemingly obscured-even brutified-man's inner, higher nature. This is why he said in *Walden* that "most men live lives of quiet desperation," trying to make a living and/or attempting to reach materialistic goals conformed to by the surrounding society. This is why he personally subscribed to the poet-philosopher's life of leisurely soul-study, in the face of strong opposition from those who believed in the ethic "work, for the night is coming." Thus he shows the "positive hindrances" of civilization by exposing in *Walden* such everyday matters as food, clothing, shelter, furniture, as well as education, law, reform to the test of fitness to man's "inner necessities." The paradox of civilization, then, was that it actually "barbarized" men, since it drove them or caused them to drift farther away from awareness of their inner selves. By the same token, Thoreau contended that he had "civilized" himself by the experience of Walden, since he approached self-realization and oneness with Nature.

WALDEN (1854)

The germ of this volume is of course to be found in Thoreau's daily entries in his Journal during the two-year stay at Walden Pond, entries which attempt to capture the spontaneity of his life and experiences in Nature there. But, as pointed out, *Walden* is more than a mere record of the years 1854-47; it is that experience metaphorized by thought and revisions over the years until its appearance in 1854 (several editions of *Walden*, for example, distinguish ideas and passages altered or even added between the early and the later periods of its growth as a book). These later revisions emphasize too, of course, that *Walden* is a more structurally unified work than a simple diary of events would be.

One large area of revisions and additions, for example, which made *Walden* a sophisticated, mature work was that of symbolism and **imagery**. Thoreau had seen, for instance, that the narrative action might be condensed from two years into one and related to the four seasons. Such a structure enabled him to draw parallels upon the seasons of life itself, and to expand the symbolism of, say spring into an elaborate **metaphor** of purification and rebirth. Also, within the **episode** of spring he chooses to focus on the thaw, which amounts to dropping one's shell or skin (the thick ice on the pond melts, as does the snow, flowing away to nourish new plants; flowers and trees and insects emerge from seed or shell), just as he emphasizes throughout the reptilian **imagery** to establish the idea of leaving an old, discontented, "barbarized" life and seeking a freshened, new existence. In his revisions he also elaborated on the day, which like the year had its seasons-especially morning, that most essential "waking" time: "only that day dawns to which we are fully awake." The most insistent symbol in *Walden* is of course the pond, which represents that inner, deeper self that man seeks to know.

"ON THE DUTY OF CIVIL DISOBEDIENCE" (1849)

The incident which precipitated this essay was Thoreau's arrest in July 1846 for refusal to pay his poll tax. Indeed, he had not paid tax since 1842, but on this occasion Sam Staples, the town jailor who would be required to pay Thoreau's tax if he did not, imprisoned him (he was at Walden at the time). He stayed in jail for only one night because friends paid his tax for him, as they did subsequently also. One night's stay in jail, though, however interesting, did not permit Thoreau to put the tax to a test. Furthermore, he had long been interested in the rights and responsibilities of the individual in relation to government (he considered this in *A Week on the Concord and Merrimack Rivers*, which he was at that time writing), and in 1848 he had lectured at the Concord Lyceum twice on civil disobedience. He makes clear his anti-slavery position in *Walden*, too (for his views on civil disobedience were grounded in his outrage at a government that permitted slavery and "overran unjustly" foreign countries such as Mexico), suggesting refusal to recognize the authority of "the State which buys and sells men, women, and children, like cattle at the door of its senate-house."

In this essay Thoreau is also invoking Transcendentalist principles of moral law, the idea that a man's conscience is his first guide; for the Transcendentalists felt that their materialistically geared society encouraged apathy, complacency, passivity, even moral cowardice in its citizens. In the place of these undesirable qualities Thoreau wished for individual citizens who would make up a "wise minority," offering against their government when they believed it to be wrong a passive resistance which was yet not so passive, since it was designed to clog the machinery of, place obstacles in the path of, the government. These ideas have of course come down to the present, from Mahatma Gandhi's philosophy through to the present civil rights crisis in America.

DETAILED SUMMARY: WALDEN

CHAPTER I: ECONOMY

Thoreau begins the now-famous *Walden* very directly: "When I wrote the following pages, or rather the bulk of them, I lived alone, in the woods, a mile from any neighbor, in a house which I had built myself, on the shore of Walden Pond, in Concord, Massachusetts ... I should not obtrude my affairs so much on the notice of my readers if very particular inquiries had not been made by my townsmen concerning my mode of life ..."

COMMENT:

Although such an opening—and the method of presentation throughout *Walden*—suggests the spontaneity of sheer reporting, that Thoreau claims, this was not actually the case: *Walden* went through at least seven versions (revisions) before publication, and the "bulk" of the work which Thoreau may have written during his stay at the pond was either put down in the journal he had kept regularly since leaving Harvard, or was recorded in the first and roughest draft of *Walden*. It is important to establish, then, at the outset, that *Walden* is not merely a verbatim report of two years in the woods but is the creative expression of such an experience *reflected* upon between 1845 and 1857.

The author apologizes for using the first person—"I"—adding that "I should not talk so much about myself if there were anybody else whom I knew so well. Unfortunately, I am confined to this theme by the narrowness of my experience. Moreover, I, on my side, require of every writer, first or last, a simple and sincere account of his own life, and not merely what he has heard of other men's lives." He further comments that "perhaps these pages are more particularly addressed to poor students."

COMMENT:

Thoreau's remarks about use of first person narrative are clearly exaggerated. First of all, he understood the value of the "I" in developing an atmosphere or authenticity and directness. Secondly, he is introducing the ironic tone he will sustain throughout, by statements such as there was no one "else whom I knew so well," or the "narrowness" of his experience (since, of course, he believed this experience to have been the most broadening one of his whole life). Furthermore, in referring to his prerequisite of "sincerity" in other writers as well as in himself, he is striking the chord of "non-conformity," as opposed to following the crowd ("merely what he has heard of other men's lives"): the idea of non-conformity is of course basic to all of Thoreau's thought. Finally in mentioning that his pàges are dedicated especially to "poor students," he is drawing upon both biographical fact and cherished belief: he himself had been a poor student, and indeed, had been plagued all his life by the dulling necessity of making a living; yet his ideal for a life well-lived—the life of a poet/philosopher—had remained in the face of all obstacles and criticism that of the "poor student," or. defined on a higher plane by Emerson in "The American Scholar," the man who simplifies his life in order that he may have energy and leisure to reflect "complexly" upon life. Thus the very title of the first chapter, "Economy," while certainly referring to the actual economies Thoreau practiced at Walden and at other times, is also ironic in its suggestion of *spiritual* economies forced upon the author by the world outside, his temporary withdrawal to the woods in order to revitalize his spirit and realize his inner self.

Thereupon Thoreau launches his major attack upon his own American civilization—its materialistic values and its unthinking work ethic—preparing the ground for his own stripping-down of such values through defining what are the actual "necessaries" of life after all: again he speaks with seeming naiveté, saying it is necessary before proceeding to say a little about the people of New England, whose young men, he remarks, "might have seen with clearer eyes what field they were called to labor in." That is, "men labor under a mistake. The better part of the man is soon ploughed into the soil for compost. By a seeming fate, commonly called necessity, they are employed, as it says in an old book, laying up treasures which moth and rust will corrupt and thieves break through and steal." Most men, to Thoreau, "are so occupied with the factitious cares and superfluously coarse labors of life that its finer fruits cannot be plucked by them." They are, in short, burdened like "machines" with merely making a living.

COMMENT:

The ideas of "vocation," the choice of it, and of making a living, the necessity of it, were very dear to Thoreau. From the time he graduated from Harvard in 1837 he was subject to questions and criticism about his own refusal to choose a vocation suitable for a Harvard man—divinity, law, or scholarly teaching, lecturing and writing would have been approved professions at the time. Similarly, since he lacked a background of wealth, he was confronted from the first with making a living; but he resented all money-making activities—from working in his father's pencil manufacturing concern, to supervising Emerson's household during his frequent absences, to the occupation of surveyor—which inevitably, he asserted, infringed upon his individuality, sapped his mental energy, and thus removed him farther from his goal of realizing the inner self. When Thoreau claims that "the mass of men lead lives of quiet desperation," then, he is also poignantly identifying himself with this mäss of men.

Thoreau therefore poses the important question as to what are the real necessities of life, things essential to people anywhere, answering the question with a short list: food, shelter, clothing and fuel. These necessities he contrasts to the luxuries or comforts man thinks he must pursue but which are in reality hindrances to his finding his higher nature. Yet he sees it as practically inevitable, especially in urban life, for men to get caught in the trap of see long after these frivolous luxuries after they have fulfilled the basic needs; furthermore, even in filling basic needs such as clothing and shelter men tend to follow each other like sheep, conforming to what is fashion or approved form rather than selecting what is functional or aesthetically pleasing.

Thoreau's solution to what he saw as the problem of modem civilized man was to take to the woods, in order to learn more about the world and man and himself: "My purpose, in going „ to Walden Pond was not to live cheaply nor to live dearly there, but to transact some private business with the fewest obstacles. His "private business" was to search his own soul, to find a self partly through the strict simplification of the externals of existence. His "capital" for the venture is quite in contrast to the fashion-conscious civilization he has left behind: his clothes are simple and sturdy; the hut he constructs is functional for all seasons (he describes in detail the building of this structure, 10 by 15 feet, with two large windows, a brick fireplace, a closet, one door, a shingled roof, which cost a total of $28.12 1/2); his diet (also detailed) is unadorned, vegetarian yet tasty. On the building he did all the work himself (studying masonry, for example, to build the fireplace), financing it by a gardening project—especially beans—and also earning some money from surveying, carpentry, and day-labor. (He seems to take an especial delight in the fact that his hut cost him less than a year's rent for a student at Cambridge College, remarking that "the student who wishes for a shelter can obtain one for a lifetime at an expense not greater than the rent which he now pays annually.") All Thoreau's earnings and expenditures, diet, furnishings, are here detailed.

Thus he discovered that he could support himself for a year. on the earnings of six weeks, leaving himself free for study and reflection. Again he stresses the non-conformist motives, instead of motives of "laziness," (i.e., escapism) in selecting such a life, remarking, as was true, that he had once worked as a school teacher but disliked it because "my expenses were ... out of proportion to my income, for I was obliged to dress and train, not to say think and believe, accordingly, and I lost my time into the bargain."

COMMENT:

Here again what Thoreau really means by "expenses" is an expense of spirit, the frustration of conforming thoughts and beliefs as well as appearance to the customary forms. Thus imprisoned rather than free, ne lost precious time which could have been devoted to probing the life of the spirit through communion with Nature (since he has decided, partly through theory and partly through practice, that living close to Nature is living close to God and carries with it the approach to unity and purity of self).

CHAPTER II: WHERE I LIVED, AND WHAT I LIVED FOR

Thoreau begins, "At a certain season of our life we are accustomed to consider every spot as the possible site of a house. I have thus surveyed the country on every side within a dozen miles of where I live. In imagination I have bought all the farms in succession, for all were to be bought, and I knew their price." Thus he describes how he got to know each of the farmers and their lands, becoming known in the neighborhood as a "sort of real-estate broker." Thoreau in fact became interested in really buying one farm, the Hollowell farm, attracted by "its complete retirement... its bounding on the river ... the gray color and ruinous state of the house and barn, and the dilapidated fences, which put such an interval between me and the last occupant... the hollow and lichen-covered apple trees ... but above all, the recollection I had of it from my earliest voyages up the river, when the house was concealed behind a dense grove of red maples...."

COMMENT:

Thoreau continues by saying that he especially wanted to buy this farm to enjoy its "advantages" outlined above, before the owner Hollowell had completed his "improvements" such as repair, getting out rocks, cutting down the hollow trees; in short, the chief virtue of such a site for the author was its isolation, just as its principal "crop" for him would have been spiritual. But even this sort of purchase seemed too binding, for Thoreau closes by commenting, "But I would say to my fellow's, once for all, As long as possible live tree and uncommitted. It makes little difference whether you are Committed to a "farm or the county jail."

Thoreau stresses the unfinished and open quality of the cabin in which he took up his abode on Independence Day, July 4, 1845: "merely a defense against the rain," lacking a chimney or plastering, it had "a clean and airy look, especially in the morning." He is enchanted with its "auroral character," comparing it in remembrance to "a certain house on a mountain which I had visited a year before. This was an airy and unplastered cabin, fit to entertain a travelling god, and where a goddess might trail her garments." Most important to him is that the fresh air remains inside his house.

COMMENT:

Thoreau is actually eulogizing the "auroral character" of his abode here and in the passages following, drawing a moral from Nature (as he was inclined to do from Transcendental principle and from personal belief). The freshness of the morning encourages awareness and simplicity and purity. all conducive to discovering the inner self, to feeling spiritual union with the whole cosmos. [Thoreau's idea of "simplicity," sometimes referred to as his "doctrine of simplicity," is that one's *style* of life must be simplified—i.e., the physical characteristics of everyday life—in order that, the spirit be freed to philosophize and find itself. In other words, simplicity to Thoreau did not suggest a bovine character of mental life; rather, he felt that a simple, peaceful pastoral setting was the ideal cradle for birth of complex thoughts.] Thus he asserts that "every morning was a cheerful invitation to make my life of equal simplicity, and I may say innocence, with Nature herself ... Morning brings back the heroic ages ... The morning, which is the most memorable season of the day, is the awakening hour. Then there is least somnolence in us; and for an hour, at least, some part of us awakes which slumbers all the rest of the day and night." It is plain that "morning" takes on symbolic, creative significance" for him, suggestive of rebirth: "Poetry and art, and the fairest and most memorable of the actions of men, date from such an hour." His message, therefore, spoken alike to himself and his audience, is that "we must learn to reawaken and keep ourselves awake, not by mechanical aids, but by an infinite expectation of the dawn, which does not forsake us in our soundest sleep."

Again Thoreau returns to the "business" he had do transact at Walden (mentioned in "Economy") in stating "I went to the woods because I wished to live deliberately, to front only the essential facts of life, and see if I could not learn what it had to teach, and not, when I came to die, discover that I had not lived. I did not wish to live what was not life, living is so dear; nor did I wish to practice resignation, unless it was quite necessary ... I wanted to live deep and suck out all the marrow of life, ... to drive life into a corner, and reduce it to its lowest terms, and, if it proved to be mean, why then to get the whole and genuine meanness of it, and publish its meanness to the world; or if it were sublime, to know it by experience, and be able to give a true account of it in my next excursion. For most men, it appears to me. are in a strange uncertainty about it, whether it is "of the devil or of God...."

COMMENT:

This passage contains the core of Thoreau's intent and belief, both in living and writing *Walden*. All the thoughts contained here are elaborated upon in the chapters following in *Walden*. It seems clear from this passage that Thoreau's withdrawal from civilized urban society was, even in his mind, a temporary and somewhat artificial one, rather than escapism, as some critics have supposed; for him it had become "necessity" to front the essentials of life, to arrange his circumstances so that he could do this—the earnestness and pathos of this desire are seen in "I did not wish to live what was not life, living is so dear." It is a rather natural confrontation for a thoughtful young man of 28.

By "resignation" Thoreau means giving oneself up to the humdrum, dulling existence of merely acquiring material possessions, of only earning a living. Note that "he adds, "unless it was quite necessary." In truth, Thoreau, like most men, was compelled frequently throughout his life both before and after Walden to resign himself to earning his bread. Knowledge of this fact, knowledge of what seems here to be his foreshadowing awareness and fear of it, is what indeed makes *Walden* more poignant than an unreflecting autobiographical report of a two-year sojourn in the woods could ever be. In the period after 1845-47, therefore, Thoreau felt himself sometimes trapped in just the way he cautions man not to allow himself to be, by civilized society, so that the record of his experience which evolved during these years and was finally presented in 1854 contains also his depressions and his struggle to regain the spiritual exaltation he felt at Walden.

CHAPTER III: READING

Thoreau begins by asserting, "With a little more deliberation in the choice of their pursuits, all men would perhaps become essentially students and observers, for certainly their nature and destiny are interesting to all alike. In accumulating property for ourselves or our posterity, in founding a family or a state, or acquiring fame even, we are mortal; but in dealing with truth we are immortal, and need fear no change nor accident." His own choice of residence, therefore, is more favorable to reading and meditation than a university; while he has access to fewer books, and does not have full time at present to devote to reading (since he has had his house to "finish, and his beans to hoe), the time he spends with these, books is most fruitful.

Thoreau praises the ancient "heroic" books, such as those of Homer, Virgil and Aeschylus, as ideal reading material, inasmuch as we may "in some measure emulate their heroes, and consecrate morning hours to their pages?' (We recall that to the author the morning hours are the most precious, because it is then he feels most mentally alert.) He further approves reading these classics in the original languages: "it is worth the expense of youthful days and costly hours, if you learn only some words of an ancient language ...." The reader must, of course, bring to a book the same spirit of deliberation and effort that the author expended in writing it. Thoreau also cites the "scriptures of the nation"—the Bible, the *Vedas* and *Zendavestas* of the Hindus, other sacred books, Dante and Shakespeare—as worthwhile reading.

He laments the fact, however, that great books are read by so few, asking for example, "What does our Concord culture amount to?" His main point here is that "even the college-bred and so-called liberally educated men here and elsewhere have really little or no acquaintance with the English classics." Too many men regard reading as a practical convenience, using this faculty as they have developed it merely for daily newspaper perusal or for "easy reading." Thoreau cites an amusing anecdote: "Most men are satisfied if they read or hear read, and perchance have been convicted by the wisdom of one good book, the Bible, and for the rest of their lives vegetate and dissipate their faculties in what is called easy reading. There is a work in several volumes in our Circulating Library entitled Little Reading, which I thought referred to a town of that name which I had not been to."

COMMENT:

It should be noted that in suggesting that with more deliberate choice of profession, "all men would perhaps become essentially students and observers," Thoreau is once again (as he does throughout) elevating the position of the "scholar" in society, the man who chooses a life of reading and meditation; he wishes to be for the most part a poet-philosopher. Thoreau had been influenced in this view by Emerson and his famous essay "The American Scholar," first presented before Thoreau's graduating class at Harvard and addressed to young men like Thoreau: Emerson too urged the casting aside of professions of business—devotion to the acquisition of material items, that is—in favor of a scholarly life. The scholar, Emerson said on another occasion, "is the favorite of Heaven and earth, the excellency of his country, the happiest of men ... His successes are occasions of the purest joy to all men."

Also, this chapter is an extension of a previous article wherein Thoreau had discussed literature and "scripture." Literature was one way of borrowing from the past, a source of inspiration for present living. It was his intention to combine such inspiration from the past and the great with his present experiment in living: from all these sources assimilated into his consciousness would come, he believed, the divine revelation of living experience. Nature, however, was still the main avenue to the inner life; and his next chapter continues the "experiment" by discussing "Sounds."

Thoreau closes the chapter by specifically criticizing New England for its hypocrisy in the face of cultural expansion. "We boast that we belong to the nineteenth century and are making the most rapid strides of any nation. But consider how little this village does for its own culture." [Concord is his example.] He asserts that there are not decent libraries or secondary and adult schools in all of New England, since the community lavishes expenditure on "almost any article of bodily aliment or ailment than on our mental aliment." On the contrary, a rich country should be the first to patronize the fine arts. Accusing New England of provincialism, then, he issues a challenge: "To act collectively is according to the spirit of our institutions; and I am confident that, as our circumstances are more flourishing, our means are greater than the nobleman's. New England can hire all the wise men in the world to come and teach her, and board them round the while, and not be provincial at all. That is the *uncommon* school we want. Instead of noblemen, let us have noble villages of men. If it is necessary, omit one bridge over the river, go round a little there, and throw one arch at least over the darker gulf of ignorance which surrounds us."

COMMENT:

Even back in his college days Thoreau had written urging, for example, that the state offer compulsory public education. He always subscribed to legislation helpful to the general public welfare. In the tone of the above passage, however, there is also a hint of the individualist who would refuse to pay his poll-tax on the principle that his community's government was not as good as it could be: this incident is described and reflected upon in his essay, "On the Duty of Civil Disobedience."

CHAPTER IV: SOUNDS

Just as the chapter "Reading" describes the discipline of using the past for inspiration, so "Sounds" suggests the discipline of "reading" Nature. Thoreau's sense of hearing seems to have been acute, providing him with many insights into the sounds of living Nature. He asks, "Will you be a reader, a student merely, or a seer? Read your fate, see what is before you, and walk on into futurity." Although the first summer was partly occupied with manual work which kept him from reading much, there were also times when he "could not afford to sacrifice the bloom of the present moment to any work, whether of the head or hands." Thus he would sometimes sit in his sunny doorway all the morning, listening and thinking, contemplating the forest, birds, animals, the distant highway. He describes some of the local wildlife, then, upon hearing a far-off train whistle, he launches into a digression on the railroad, the changes it has brought to life and to commerce, acknowledging that commercial life has its advantages as well as its drawbacks. He goes on to speak of other sounds which are a part of his daily life—church bells, the distant lowing of a cow, the whippoorwills chanting, and amusingly, owls: "I rejoice that there are owls. Let them do the idiotic and maniacal hooting for men. It is a sound admirably suited to swamps and twilight woods which no day illustrates, suggesting a vast and undeveloped nature which men have not recognized. They represent the stark twilight and unsatisfied thoughts which all have."

COMMENT:

This chapter is the clearest indication so far of Thoreau's conviction that an acute awareness of the motions of Nature, meditated upon, was the entrance to a spiritual world linked to the world of Nature. The gateway to the life of the spirit—the inner life he sought— was through blending oneself into Nature as far as possible.

WALDEN

TEXTUAL ANALYSIS

CHAPTERS 5 - 8

CHAPTER V: SOLITUDE

This chapter continues the idea of communion with nature, beginning by "this is a delicious evening, when the whole body is one sense, and imbibes delight through every pore. I go and come with a strange liberty in Nature, a part of herself." It is an unusually "congenial" evening, with bullfrogs trumping, sounds of whippoorwills, a cool breeze. He returns home to find visitors have left calling cards-flowers, evergreen, a name penciled on a yellow walnut leaf or a chip. He remarks on the solitude of his place, with the nearest neighbor a mile distant, with very few travellers stopping to disturb "the black kernel of night." He comments that perhaps "men are generally still a little, afraid of the dark, though the witches are all hung, and Christianity and candles have been introduced." At the same time, Thoreau insists that his solitude was not morbid or melancholy, for "there can be no very black melancholy to him who lives in the midst of Nature and has his senses still." He sees even the rain as a source of cheer-nourishment for his beans-rather than a dreary occasion, saying that some of his pleasantest hours were spent during the long rain storms of the spring or the fall, confined as he was to his house, "soothed by their ceaseless roar and pelting."

When people ask him if he is lonesome where he lives, therefore, he feels like replying, "This whole earth which we inhabit is but a point in space. How far apart, think you, dwell the two most distant inhabitants of yonder star, the breadth of whose disk cannot be appreciated by our instruments? Why should I feel lonely? Is not our planet in the Milky Way? This which you put seems to me not to be the most important question. What sort of space is that which separates a man from his fellows and makes him solitary? I have found that no exertion of the legs can bring two minds much nearer to one another."

Comment

This was indeed a "most important question" to Thoreau, the question of communication-even communion, according to his ideal for friendship-between men. Friendship, he believed, should involve just this sort of communion-exchange of thoughts, ideas, philosophy-between men who sought their own higher nature, who were aware of the inner life. It was a very high standard for human relations that Thoreau set for himself and others; and his biographers generally picture him as inclined toward few rather than many close friendships. Even the exalted Emerson could not measure up to Thoreau's ideal for friendship, for he complained on more than one occasion of not being able to reach that higher plateau of communication with Emerson, his mentor.

Furthermore, Thoreau continues, there is a kind of aloneness which is always with us, in the sense that we sometimes step outside our own thoughts or actions and become spectators: "By a conscious effort of the mind we can stand aloof from actions and their consequences ... I only know myself as a human entity; the scene, so to speak, of thoughts and affections; and am sensible of a certain doubleness by which I can stand as remote from myself as from another. However intense my experience, I am conscious of the presence and criticism of a part of me, which, as it were, is not a part of me, but spectator, sharing no experience, but taking note of it." Thus Thoreau finds it "wholesome to be alone the greater part of the time."

He even insists that we often see our close associates too often, making society "cheap" and "not having had time to acquire any new value for each other." In addition, when men do their daily work, they are in a sense alone.

He closes the chapter by evoking again this kindredness which he feels with Nature. "I have a great deal of company in my house; especially in the morning," he says, and cites the company of the dandelion, the loon, the sun. "I am no more lonely than the Mill Brook, or a weathercock, or the north star, or the south wind, or an April shower, or a January thaw, or the first spider in a new house." Thus he makes it clear that he thinks of Nature as almost "animate," its fellows as much companions as human beings.

CHAPTER VI: VISITORS

Perhaps desiring to qualify his remarks on solitude and companionship, Thoreau asserts, "I think that I love society as much as most, and am ready enough to fasten myself like a bloodsucker for the time to any full-blooded man that comes in my way. I am naturally no hermit, but might possibly sit out the sturdiest frequenter of the bar-room, if my business called me thither." He describes his ways of entertaining company at Walden. "I had three chairs in my house; one for solitude, two for friendship, three for society. When visitors came in larger and unexpected numbers there was but the third chair for them all, but they generally economized the room by standing up." He observes that our houses are in general too large for us, that he was able to entertain 25 or 30 people at a time in his little house without a crowded feeling.

He admits however that "big thoughts" need space. "One inconvenience I sometimes experienced in so small a house, the difficulty of getting to a sufficient distance from my guest when we began to utter the big thoughts in big words. You want room for your thoughts to get into sailing trim and run a course or two before they make their port … If we are merely loquacious and loud talkers, then we can afford to stand very near together, cheek by jowl, and feel each other's breath; but if we speak reservedly and thoughtfully, we want to be farther apart, that all animal heat and moisture may have a chance to evaporate." He concedes then that his best room was his "withdrawing room, always ready for company, on whose carpet the sun rarely fell, … the pine wood behind my house."

When only one guest came, he shared a simple meal; more company brought no mention of food, and Thoreau states (in the same gently ironic tone which pervades this chapter, resulting in a certain charm of written style which is characteristic of Thoreau) that his reputation as a host never suffered from such "omissions." He relates a story about the visit of Winslow, governor of the Plymouth Colony, to the Village of Chief Massasoit to illustrate this view of entertaining. He had, in fact, more visitors at Walden than during any other period in his life (a bit misleading, since he adds, "I mean that I had some"); furthermore, few came on trivial business. One of Thoreau's favorite visitors was a Canadian wood-chopper and postmaker: Thoreau calls him a "true Homeric or Paphlagonian man" who has heard of Homer, reads books on rainy days, but is not corrupted by civilization. He has a "slumbering" mind, its seeds not yet awakened to discipline of expression. "To him Homer was a great writer, though what his writing was about he did not know. A more simple and natural man it would be hard to find. Vice and disease, which cast such a sombre moral hue over the world, seemed to have hardly any existence for him... He interested me because he was so quiet and solitary and so happy withal; a well of good humor and contentment which overflowed at his eyes. His mirth was without alloy ... In him the animal man chiefly was developed. In physical endurance and contentment he was cousin to the pine and the rock ... But the intellectual and what is called spiritual man in him were slumbering as in an infant." This man refuses to play a part in the world; people who get to know him simply watch him unfold. He was so humble and simple that "humility was no distinct quality in him." He did not wish to change the world, for he truly liked it as hit was (and as he knew it). However, "there was a certain positive originality, however slight, to be detected in him, and I occasionally observed that he was thinking for himself and expressing his own opinion, a phenomenon so rare that I would any day walk ten miles to observe it."

Comment

It is possible that, as he says, Thoreau did wonder whether the woodchopper was "wise as Shakespeare or as simply ignorant as a child." He seems to be exploring his own views here on what can be called a "primitive" type of person. He stresses and admires the Canadian's great simplicity and lack of guile; at the same time he believes - rather, he wants to believe - that the man is possessed of latent intellectual and spiritual powers, since these elements would make him fully kindred to Thoreau. We can make a distinction here between the terms "primitive" and "pastoral," though: primitive, or primitivism (a term which is applied by some critics, rejected by others, with respect to Thoreau), refers to man living in a practically animal or savage state, without any overlay of outside civilization, his physical environs crude, his mental life at least undetermined; pastoral, however (and "pastoralism" has also been applied to Thoreau), suggests rural life, perhaps of farming, lived by men with some experience of civilization who choose the pastoral life for what it has to offer them, in simplicity, in potential for meditation and spiritual growth. It is probably the pastoral rather than the strictly primitive life which Thoreau elevates in *Walden* and in his admiration of the woodchopper.

His other guests included travellers, beggars, even a simple-minded pauper, whose "half wit" causes him to observe wryly that "with respect to wit, I learned that there was not much difference between the half and the whole." The half-wit presented Thoreau "a **metaphysical** puzzle ... I have rarely met a fellowman on such promising ground, - it was so simple and sincere and so true all that he said." (Here again we might infer that Thoreau's own powers of intellect and his obsessive urge to simplicity may be overestimating the "truth" of the half-wit's words.) Runaway slaves too stopped rather frequently at Thoreau's place; he always helped them northward [Later in life Thoreau became quite involved with the abolitionist cause.] There were also women and young children from the towns, walking for pleasure in the woods, and a lot of working men on their days off - "honest pilgrims" seeking the woods for "freedom's sake."

CHAPTER VII: THE BEAN-FIELD

Thoreau's one concentrated labor of the summer was growing beans, of which he had planted two and a half acres. He cannot quite explain to himself what seems to be, as they progress, almost the spiritual necessity of growing them. "What was the meaning of this so steady and self-respecting, this small Herculean labor, I knew not. I came to love my rows, my beans, though so many more than I wanted. They attached me to the earth, and so I got strength ... What shall I learn of beans or beans of me? I cherish them, I hoe them, early and late I have an eye to them, and this is my day's work." He pauses to reflect that he was brought to this very place, this very pond, when he was but four years old, and that "tonight my flute has waked the echoes over that very water." Then he continues to describe in some detail what he learned of bean husbandry, how he uncovered arrowheads and other relics of the ancient Indian cultivators of that same ground where his beans were growing. Sometimes on "gala days" the towns would fire guns, causing him to reflect on the preservation of the "liberties of Massachusetts" and of the nation, and to return to his labor "cheerfully with a calm trust in the future."

Thoreau itemizes (with a quaint grace) the commercial usefulness of his bean crop, in terms of "outgoes" ($14.72 1/2) and "income" ($8.71 1/2), the total income from his beans and other vegetables set at $23.44. He is proud of his actual success at farming, but it is clear that his profit therein has been chiefly spiritual, upon which he comments at length, observing first that "those summer days which some of my contemporaries devoted to the fine arts in Boston or Rome, and others to contemplation in India, and others to trade in London or New York, I thus, with the other farmers of New England, devoted to husbandry." But his "further experience" was that he said to himself. "I will not plant beans and corn with so much industry another summer, but such seeds, if the seed is not lost, as sincerity, truth, simplicity, faith, innocence, and the like, and see if they will not grow in this soil, even with less toil and manurance, and sustain me, for surely it has not been exhausted for these crops."

Comment

It is clear that the symbolism of roots and seeds in Nature and in his own nature figures largely here in Thoreau's thinking. He loved the beans because they attached him to the earth; in other words, they increased his sense of kindredness with Nature. The actual seeds become further seeds of virtue in his mind because they symbolize the potential harvest of spending these months in solitude and constant communion with Nature; he realizes, however, that the virtues he aspires to, the exalted inner life, will be more difficult to produce than the actual bean crop.

He closes, not surprisingly, by linking farming-husbandry-to the past, claiming that "ancient poetry and mythology suggest, at least, that husbandry was once a sacred art; but it is pursued with irreverent haste and heedlessness by us, our object being to have large farms and large crops merely. We have no festival, nor procession, nor ceremony ..." Returning to his bean crop, he attempts to grasp the greater implications: "This broad field which I have looked at so long looks not to me as the principal cultivator, but away from me to influences more genial to it, which water and make it green. These beans have results which are not harvested by me."

Comment

Thoreau here is elevating the profession of farming, especially by citing ancient authority that husbandry was formerly considered a sacred art. This is why he speaks of the "true husbandman," devoted more to the studied cultivation rather than the produce of his fields, as opposed to the modern farmer who is as obsessed with material gain as his businessman counterpart in the towns. This is again Thoreau's emphasis on the pastoral way of life as most conducive to self-realization, and to communion with Nature so vital to that inner spiritual discovery: for Thoreau, Nature and the God-like in man are forever intermingled.

CHAPTER VIII: THE VILLAGE

Sometimes after hoeing or studying (reading and writing) in the morning Thoreau would bathe himself in the pond, then walk to the village. He says, "as I walked in the woods to see the birds and squirrels, so I walked in the village to see the men and boys ...." He also went to hear some of the gossip which went on "incessantly" there. Yet after visiting with people whose company he cared about (avoiding the gossipers as much as possible, as well as the signs of material worlds - the dry goods store, the tavern, the tailor-hung along the streets to allure him and others), he always looked forward to returning to his haven. "It was very pleasant, when I stayed late in town, to launch myself into the night, especially if it was dark and tempestuous, and set sail from some bright village parlor or lecture room, with a bag of rye or Indian meal upon my shoulder, for my snug harbor in the woods ...." He comments upon how well he could find his way in the dark, that he often would direct visitors in the woods who had stayed until dark and were unable to find their way.

Comment

Here again Thoreau chooses to emphasize the symbolic significance of being lost in the woods. "Every man has to learn the points of compass again as often as he awakes, whether from sleep or any abstraction. Not till we are lost, in other words, not till we have lost the world, do we begin to find ourselves, and realize where we are and the infinite extent of our relations." His idea of course is that he himself had to lose the civilized world in withdrawal to Walden before he could find himself, his inner spiritual self. There is a hint here too of the symbolic meaning of the pond, representing that inner self he went in search of-for he always returns to the pond, to live, to meditate, suggesting that a man, for inner peace, must always lose the world to some extent and turn inward to his own personal resources.

He relates in this chapter how, upon going to the village to pick up a shoe at the cobbler's shop one afternoon in the summer of 1845, he was arrested and kept in jail overnight, because he "did not pay a tax to, or recognize the authority of, the state that buys and sells men, women, and children, like cattle at the door of its senate-house." (He is protesting the institution of human slavery, existing then within the bounds of his state of Massachusetts.) He concludes that "wherever a man goes, men will pursue and paw him with their dirty institutions, and if they can, constrain him to belong to their desperate odd-fellow society." [His protest toward this was formalized in the famous essay "On the Duty of Civil Disobedience," first published in 1849; this is why he says, "as I have related elsewhere," since the treatise was published before *Walden* was.]

Thoreau notes in fact that he has never been molested by anyone except the government, that he "had no lock nor bolt but for the desk which held my papers, not even a nail to put over my latch or windows." He never locked his doors, yet his house was respected by private individuals. He closes with advice to those who govern to shun punishments and love virtue; then the people will be virtuous. "The virtues of a superior man are like the wind; the virtues of a common man are like the grass; the grass, when the wind passes over it, bends."

CHAPTER IX: THE PONDS

When he was not hoeing or studying, Thoreau found other diversions such as picking delicious huckleberries, joining a silent fisherman on the pond, or often on a late, warm evening, sitting in his boat playing the flute. Sometimes, too, having returned from the village and visiting, he would fish in the moonlight, for the next day's meal, "serenaded" by owls and foxes or the "creaking note" of some bird. His real intent in this Chapter, however, is to describe the scenery of Walden and the other ponds around. "The scenery of Walden is on a humble scale, and, though very beautiful, does not approach to grandeur .... yet this pond is so remarkable for its depth and purity as to merit a particular description." Thereupon he details the "deep green well" which is Walden, although he adds, as to its color, that "lying between the earth and the heavens, it partakes of the color of both." The water is so transparent that you can see the bottom at 25 or 30 feet, as well as schools of perch and shiners as you paddle over it. (He relates the incident of losing his axe through an ice hole in winter and perceiving it at the bottom some 25 feet, he was able to retrieve it.) Walden's shore is made up of smooth rounded white stones like paving stones, except for a few short sandy beaches. The pond rises and falls, but in a pattern which he cannot determine, although he notes that its sister ponds, Flints' and White, respond similarly.

There are other ponds in the vicinity: Flints', known otherwise as Sandy Pond, covers 197 acres; there is also Goose Pond, Fair Haven Pond, and White Pond, which he considers to be the most beautiful, although he loves Walden best. He describes each pond in some detail, and speaks of them as lakes, "the landscape's most beautiful and expressive feature." But especially he describes how Walden served him well in all seasons, providing his drinking water as well as fish, and attracting to it other forms of wildlife. He is concerned to picture Walden's changing, seasonal beauty, concluding, "Nevertheless, of all the characters I have known, perhaps Walden wears best, and best preserves its purity. Many men have been likened to it, but few deserve that honor."

Comment

Critics tend to agree that the seasons of Walden pond are to be likened to the seasons of Thoreau's spiritual life; and it does seem to emerge especially in this chapter that Thoreau thought of the pond as his essential self (and the shore, perhaps, his actual outer self). It might follow, therefore, that through "discipline" such as cultivating beans (whose seeds represent "virtues," we recall, and whose roots attach him to the earth), Thoreau expects to make this actual outer self (the earthly one: the shore) more satisfying, more in tune with the pristine inner self of the pond.

CHAPTER X: BAKER FARM

This chapter contains an account of his journeying to Fair Haven for an afternoon of fishing and being forced by a sudden rainstorm to take refuge at Baker Farm, a farm inhabited and worked by John Field, an Irish laboring man, with his wife and several children. He sees Field as "an honest, hard-working, but shiftless man plainly," whose wife struggles to cook "successive dinners" on an ancient stove. Talking to Field "as if he were a philosopher, or desired to be one," Thoreau tried to convert him to his own simplified way of life, but without success, since the laborer, though poor, was not inclined to give up what he had already grubbed out of the ground. They go fishing together, and Field's luck remains "bad" while Thoreau catches a fair string of fish. Thoreau laments the crudeness and narrowness of a life such as John Field's, reflecting how "men come tamely home at night only from the next field or street, where their household echoes haunt, and their life pines because it breathes its own breath over again; their shadows morning and evening reach farther than their daily steps. We should come home from far, from adventures, and perils, and discoveries every day, with new experience and character." But this is a life of the spirit and the mind which the Thoreaus, not the John Fields necessarily, aspire to and sometimes reach. John Field, Thoreau reluctantly concludes, was born to be poor physically and spiritually.

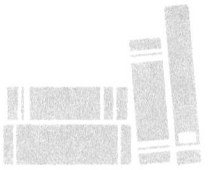

WALDEN

TEXTUAL ANALYSIS

CHAPTERS 9 - 18

CHAPTER XI: HIGHER LAWS

This chapter treats of sensuality, of the animal instinct in men. Thoreau's thoughts have been turned down these paths by glimpsing a woodchuck running across his path as he came home at night from fishing. He reflects that he "felt a strange thrill of savage delight, and was strongly tempted to seize and devour him raw; not that I was hungry then, except for that wildness which he represented." He goes on to observe that he finds dual urges within himself, nor is he distressed by them. "I found in myself, and still find, and instinct toward a higher, or, as it is named, spiritual life, as do most men, and another toward a primitive rank and savage one, and I reverence them both. I love the wild not less than the good." These urges may go back to his hunting **episodes** in childhood, he says. From a discussion of fishing and studying fowls, he goes on to explain his own vegetarian tastes, claiming that bread or potatoes do as well as meat, and with less uncleanness, his chief objection to animal foods. Furthermore, he believes that vegetarianism encourages the higher nature in man: "that every man who has ever been earnest to preserve his higher or poetic faculties in the best condition has been particularly inclined to abstain from animal food, and from much food of any kind." And indeed, his own tastes are abstemious; he believes that "water is the only drink for a wise man; wine is not so noble a liquor; and think of dashing the hopes of a morning with a cup of warm coffee, or of an evening with a dish of tea!"

Yet the real issue with Thoreau seems to be his conviction of man's sensual nature which must be controlled. "Our whole life is startlingly moral. There is never an instant's truce between virtue and vice. Goodness is the only investment that never fails." Thus it may be that he mistrusts the sensualities of food and drink and even, sometimes, music. "We are conscious of an animal in us, which awakens in proportion as our higher nature slumbers. It is reptile and sensual, and perhaps cannot be wholly expelled; like the worms which, even in life and health, occupy our bodies. Possibly we may withdraw from it, but never change its nature." "Temperance and purity," then, would be his goals, even if unattainable. And Thoreau insists that "the spirit can for the time pervade and control every member and function of the body, and transmute what in form is the grossest sensuality into purity and devotion. The generative energy, which, when we are loose, dissipates and makes us unclean, when we are continent invigorates and inspires us. Chastity is the flowering of man; and what are called Genius, Heroism, Holiness, and the like, are but various fruits which succeed it. Man flows at once to God when the channel of purity is open."

Comment

The key word here is perhaps purity, whether Thoreau speaks in terms of chastity, temperance, sloth: the more he is able to simplify his life, the more is the channel to godliness, to a life of the spirit, likely to be opened.

Thoreau here sees all sensuality as the same, whether a man eat, drink, cohabit, sleep sensually -"they are but one appetite." He admits that chastity is difficult to define, though. He affirms that "from exertion come wisdom and purity; from sloth ignorance and sensuality." Thus in a student sensuality might take the form, according to Thoreau, of a lazy mind, of lack of industry. We know chastity best, then, by its opposites. To avoid uncleanness and sins "work earnestly, though it be at cleaning a stable." He believes that silence, however, on the subject of something like the body's functions, is just another form of impurity. "We are so degraded that we cannot speak simply of the necessary functions of human nature. In earlier ages, in some countries, every function was reverently spoken of and regulated by law. Nothing was too trivial for the Hindoo law-giver, however offensive it may be to modern taste. He teaches how to eat, drink, cohabit, void excrement and urine, and the like, elevating what is mean, and does not falsely excuse himself by calling these things trifles." [As will be seen, Thoreau exhibits throughout the influence of Oriental thought and philosophy.] Every man builds his own temple which is his body, Thoreau says, according to the gods he worships. "We are all sculptors and painters, and our material is our own flesh and blood and bones. Any nobleness begins at once to refine a man's features, any meanness or sensuality to imbrute them."

CHAPTER XII: BRUTE NEIGHBORS

This chapter opens with a dialogue between a poet and a hermit, the poet a companion who came through the village to Thoreau's hut to fish with him. The poet invites Thoreau to fish, and after reflecting momentarily on the great concepts which were in his mind before the poet's arrival and trying to recapture the thoughts, he agrees to go fishing.

Comment

The "poet" apparently was William Ellery Channing the younger, Thoreau's frequent companion and first biographer. The **allusions** to Europe in the opening paragraphs ("there's nothing like it [the beautiful sky] in old paintings, nothing like it in foreign lands, - unless when we were off the coast of Spain. That's a true Mediterranean sky.") refer to Channing's educational trip to Europe, sponsored through Emerson and his friends.

Thoreau then describes in detail the different animals and birds in his area: field mice who shared his hut; birds such as the phoebe, robin, partridge; red and black ants, whose ferocious battle he watched one afternoon near his woodpile. (As in the incident of the woodchuck, in "Higher Laws," this carnage awakens Thoreau's imagination; also, he recalls, great authors of the past-Aeneas Sylvius and Olaus Magnus- who wrote of the battles of ants.) He also mentions cats, once domesticated, who course through the woods as if they were wild animals; there were the usual squirrels, raccoons, foxes and woodchucks. Thoreau had also observed the loon in particular, accumulating quite a lot of knowledge of this bird's habits, and enjoying its laugh or its dive for fish. He could also watch for hours the ducks on the pond, in fall days, "cunningly tack and veer and hold the middle of the pond, far from the sportsman."

CHAPTER XIII: HOUSE-WARMING

In October Thoreau began to get ready for winter, gathering grapes and different kinds of nuts, storing them away. It gave him great pleasure to watch, from September on, the changing landscape of fall turning into winter. He was now obliged to complete his house. Having studied masonry, he built slowly and deliberately his fireplace and chimney, for two weeks with the help of a visiting poet. Although his house is of course more comfortable in the wintering air after it is plastered, he vows it never pleased his eye so afterward as when the air was able to pass through the cracks. His pleasure in his handiwork caused him to "dream of a larger and more populous house, standing in a golden age, of enduring materials, and without gingerbread work, which shall still consist of only one room a vast, rude, substantial, primitive hall, without ceiling or plastering, with bare rafters and purlins supporting a sort of lower heaven over one's head ...."

With freezing weather the pond began to form its first layer of ice. Thoreau observes how interesting is the first thin layer, where although it was only an inch thick he could stretch out his length and look through to the bottom of the pond in shallow places. Another sign of winter's setting in was the nightly flights of geese he detected. He also keeps a record of when the ponds freeze over. His chief occupation now was the gathering of firewood and kindling; he remarks on the affection a man has for a woodpile he has himself accumulated. He adds that during the second winter at Walden he used a small cooking stove instead of his open fireplace, but that "cooking was then, for the most part, no longer a poetic, but merely a chemic process." He felt as if he had lost a companion, because "you can always see a face in the fire. The laborer, looking into it at evening, purifies his thoughts of the dross and earthiness which they have accumulated during the day."

Comment

The gathering of firewood, and the "house-warming," may be regarded as symbolic activities: Thoreau was trying to maintain "a kind of summer in the midst of winter ..." In his little house, now shingled and plastered and warm, he had now "internalized" his life. He says, "I withdrew yet farther into my shell, and endeavored to keep a bright fire both within my house and breast." He finds, nevertheless, that the winter brings with it some estrangement from Nature.

CHAPTER XIV: FORMER INHABITANTS; AND WINTER VISITORS

As Thoreau winters at Walden, weathering several snowstorms, he is obliged to conjure up the past inhabitants of the woods. One of these was Cato Ingraham, a slave who had been permitted by his owner to live in his own house in Walden Woods. Cato had intended to use the lands for his old age but "a younger and whiter speculator got them at last." Both men have been dead now any years. Also, by the corner of Thoreau's field nearest to town, an old colored woman named Zilpha had a little house where she spun linen for the townsfolk. She had a good and loud singing voice, and made Walden Woods ring with her singing. Her house and possessions were burned during the War of 1812 by some British soldiers on parole. Down the road had lived Brister Freeman, a freed slave of Squire Cummings, and his wife Fenda, who told fortunes, "yet pleasantly." Thoreau had seen Freeman's **epitaph** in Lincoln burying-ground. The apple trees Brister planted were still growing, but their fruit, because untended, was sour. Other local inhabitants were the Stratton family, at the Breed's location, "a demon not distinctly named in old mythology, who has acted a prominent and astounding part in our New England life ... New England Rum." Thoreau recalls when Breed's hut burned, about a dozen years ago, having been set fire to by mischievous boys one Election night. The latest inhabitant before Thoreau was Colonel Hugh Quiol, Irish veteran of the Napoleonic Wars. This intelligent and civilized man died shortly before Thoreau came to Walden. Thoreau remarks that, given his great curiosity about history, he would have made the colonel fight his battles all over again, had he known him.

Thoreau had few visitors during the winter season. He merely lived "snug as a meadow mouse" in his hut, or took walks into the snowbound woods, making observations on the wildlife. His poet friend William Ellery Channing the younger came, however, "through deepest snows and most dismal tempests," as well as another "welcome visitor, who at one time came through the village, through snow and rain and darkness, till he saw my lamp through the trees, and shared with me some long winter evenings." This man [he was Bronson Alcott] Thoreau calls "one of the last of the philosophers ... the man of the most faith of any alive. His words and attitude always suppose a better state of things than other men are acquainted with, and he will be the last man to be disappointed as the ages revolve."

Thoreau mentions two other visitors. "There was one other with whom I had 'solid seasons,' long to be remembered, at his house in the village, and who looked in upon me from time to time; but I had no more for society there." He also expected the

"Visitor who never comes," he says: according to the ritual set forth in the Vishnu Purana he remained at even tide in his courtyard as long as it takes to milk a cow; "I often performed this duty of hospitality, waited long enough to milk a whole herd of cows, but did not see the man approaching from the town."

Comment

The "one other" is probably Emerson. The ambiguous remark "but I had no more for society there," especially when compared to the longer, generous tributes to William Ellery Channing and Bronson Alcott, suggests the breakdown in friendship between Thoreau and Emerson.

CHAPTER XV: WINTER ANIMALS

After the ponds were fully frozen, they afforded Thoreau new and shorter routes to many points, as well as novel views of the same landscape. Sounds of the winter night included the hooting of owls, the honking of geese and especially, the "whooping" of the ice on Walden Pond (similar to the cracking of the ground by frost). He could also hear the foxes ranging over the crusted snow, and in the morning the red squirrel awakened him by running over the roof and down the sides of his house. He fed the red squirrels and the rabbits unripened sweet corn, a meal shared by the chickadees and jays. When the ground was not quite covered with snow, or later when some of the snow had melted, he saw partridges feeding at the edge of the woods; often sportsmen would lie in wait for them nearby. Also on winter mornings sometimes Thoreau heard the hounds in chase, and the sound of a hunting horn proving that men accompanied in the rear. He relates several anecdotes passed on to him by hunters-for example, one Sam Nutting, a former bear hunter. It is interesting to note that the hunters used to exchange their skins for rum in Concord village : wild-cat, deer, bear skins. He also details how the squirrels and wild mice quarrel over his supply of nuts, or how a hare who lived underneath his house startled him by her departure each morning when he got up, with her thumping as she struck her head against the floor boards in hurrying away from the human above. He concludes by remarking, "What is a country without rabbits and partridges? They are among the most simple and indigenous animal products; ancient and venerable families known to antiquity as to modern times; of the very hue and substance of Nature, nearest to leaves and to the ground."

CHAPTER XVI: THE POND IN WINTER

Sometimes after a still winter night Thoreau awoke with the impression that a question had been put to him in his sleep - "what-how-when-where?" The sense of the question, however, is dispelled in "dawning Nature, in whom all creatures live, looking in at my broad windows with serene and satisfied face, and no question on her lips. I awoke to an answered question, to Nature and daylight." Then the glory of the new day sends him forth into his morning work. He went at the difficult task of getting water, for example: he had to cut through a foot of snow, then a foot of ice, before reaching water. Sometimes he fished through the hole in the ice, like the other fishermen who might come in the early morning, with reels and lunches. He pauses to comment upon the rare beauty of the pickerel of Walden, with their colors "not green like the pines, nor gray like the stones, nor blue like the sky'" but of "flowers and precious stones, as if they were the pearls ... of the Walden water."

In order to disprove to himself the rumor that Walden Pond was bottomless, he surveyed it with care 1846; he did however find that the deepest part of the part of the pond was 102 feet, rather unusual for such a small body of water. The depth of Walden encourages him to philosophize, "What if all ponds were shallow? Would it not react on the minds of men? I am thankful that this pond was made deep and pure for a symbol. While men believe in the infinite some ponds will be thought to be bottomless." During the winter he surveyed and sounded the other ponds in the area, developing from this experience some theories on the structure of such bodies of water. Again he philosophizes that "what I have observed of the pond is no less true in ethics. It is the law of average. Such a rule of the two diameters not only guides us toward the sun in the system and the heart in man, but draws lines through the length and breadth of the aggregate of a man's particular daily behaviors and waves of life into his coves and inlets, and where they intersect will be the height or depth of his character. Perhaps we need only to know how his shores trend and his adjacent country or circumstances, to infer his depth and concealed bottom."

He describes how a hundred Irish workmen with Yankee overseers came from Cambridge to cut out ice from Walden. During 16 days they cut out large blocks of ice and stored them on the shore under layers of hay and boards. The total cut out during the whole winter was estimated to weigh 10,000 tons. Although some of it would melt during the spring and early summer, enough would remain to be shipped to warmer regions. Thoreau disliked the removal of the pond's "skin," but the ice had replaced itself within a month of completion of the job. He seems to like the idea that people of Charleston or New Orleans drink at his well, just as he himself bathes his intellect in Hindu philosophy every morning and feels that in going to his "well" for water he meets his fellows of Madras and Bombay and Calcutta: The pure Walden water is mingled with the sacred water of the Ganges."

Comment

This chapter makes especially clear Thoreau's constant intellectual search for faith, and the revelations he felt in the midst of Nature. For the question "what-how-when-where?" is answered by the living presence of Nature and its new dawn. (We recall the reiterated significance of each new morning to him.) It is an awareness of "life" in Nature which prepares him for the rebirth (of, and in "Spring") of his spirit, a rebirth which is cyclic. Man's nature is not shallow, he insists - and the analogy of deep ponds is further proof of man's potential depth (the pond as a symbol of self): any analogy of man with Nature is to Thoreau a valid one, worth philosophizing about.

CHAPTER XVII: SPRING

Thoreau observed very closely the process of the breaking up of the ice and the gradual thaw of Walden and the ponds around, a process which he describes in detail, as occurring every day on a small scale. The ice cracks and booms with temperature changes; the ice begins to be honey-combed and he can set his heel in it. With the melting of the ice and the warming air came the first plants above the now-bare ground, then the first birds. Thus the phenomenon of the thaw fascinates Thoreau: "Ere long, not only on these banks, but on every hill and plain and in every hollow, the frost comes out of the ground like a dormant quadruped from its burrow, and seeks the sea with music, or migrates to other climes in clouds. Thaw with his gentle persuasion is more than Thor with his hammer." And at last spring seems instantaneous: "The change from storm and winter to serene and mild weather, from dark and sluggish hours to bright and elastic ones, is a memorable crisis which all things proclaim. It is seemingly instantaneous at last. Suddenly an influx of light filled my house, though the evening was at hand, and the clouds of winter still overhung it, and the eaves were dripping with sleety rain." In closing, Thoreau remarks that his second year, and spring, in Walden were much like the first. He left the pond on September 6, 1847.

Comment

Clearly Thoreau has made a **metaphor** of himself, his own inner purification and rebirth, out of the thaw, just as the entire **episode** of Spring is a re-enacted myth of creation to him. (And we ought to note that this chapter contains some of his most poetically descriptive passages.) The symbolic ecstasy which Thoreau experiences from the thaw, however, is a combination of his spontaneous experience of its actuality and his later reflections on those two springs at Walden mingled with all the other spring phenomena he had ever in his life observed. Yet to him the coming of spring was no less than "the creation of Cosmos out of Chaos and the realization of the Golden Age" (thus he evokes, as always, the ancients of the written word too). Through spring he felt newly arisen as from a grave of winter (and deep thought, mixed with sluggish discontent), "free in this world, as birds in the air, disengaged from every kind of chain."

CHAPTER XVIII: CONCLUSION

Thoreau herein justifies his withdrawal to Walden for two years, beginning with "the universe is wider than our views of it": therefore let us broaden our views of the universe. He says, "I left the woods for as good a reason as I went there. Perhaps it seemed to me that I had several more lives to live, and could not spare any more time for that one." In short, he found also that he could beat a path to his hut in the woods as well as he could fall into a routine of existence in society outside-or almost as well. In any case, life in the woods now needed a freshened view of contrasting it to life outside again. His lessons learned at Walden were many and lasting, however; "I learned this, at least, by my experiment; that if one advances confidently in the direction of his dreams, and endeavors to live the life which he has imagined, he will meet with a success unexpected in common hours. He will put some things behind, will pass an invisible boundary; new, universal, and more liberal laws will begin to establish themselves around and within him; or the old laws be expanded ... and he will live with the license of a higher order of beings. In proportion as he simplifies his life, the laws of the universe will appear less complex, and solitude will not be solitude, nor poverty poverty, nor weakness weakness." What Thoreau is really praising is the essence of his stay in the woods: his own self-awareness. Thus he can say to others, "explore your own higher latitudes ...." Furthermore, do not fear your own individuality, he seems to suggest in "why level downward to our dullest perception always, and praise that as common sense? The commonest sense is the sense of men asleep, which they express by snoring." (He is again returning to the idea of man awake, in all possible ways.) And "why should we be in such desperate haste to succeed and in such desperate enterprises? If a man does not keep pace with his companions, perhaps it is because he hears a different drummer. Let him step to the music which he hears...."

Thoreau asserts that men need not "be shipwrecked on a vain reality"; that is, a man need not "turn his spring into summer. If the condition of things which we were made for is not yet, what were any reality which we can substitute?" He cites an illustrative anecdote of an artist who once lived in the ancient Indian city of Kouroo. This man desired to make a staff, deciding, "It shall be perfect in all respects, though I should do nothing else in my life." He worked on this task so long that time became unimportant, even though the city became a ruin and generations came and went by. His finished staff was indeed perfect, and he realized with some astonishment that "he had made a new system in making a staff, a world with full and fair proportions; in which, though the old cities and dynasties had passed away, fairer and more glorious ones had taken their places. And now he saw ... that, for him and his work, the former lapse of time had been an illusion .... The material was pure, and his art was pure; how could the result be other than wonderful?"

Comment

We have here in the story of the Indian artist of Kouroo a parable of Thoreau's own work, and hence, his life. His writing, such as *Walden*, was much revised before publication; furthermore, his work was often enough ill-received, requiring of him patience and faith in the individual worth of his "life-staff" in order to keep on working.

To Thoreau, perhaps, the "staff" also represents "truth," whether of his work or his life, for he continues, "rather than love, than money, than fame, give me truth. I sat at a table where were rich food and wine in abundance, and obsequious attendance, but sincerity and truth were not; and I went away hungry ...." Although his generation offers Philosophical Societies, formally acclaimed Great Men, a lot of self-congratulation, where is there just one person who has lived "a whole human life?" To live this whole human life means to be as aware as possible, to admit life's novelty. "There is an incessant influx of novelty into the world, and yet we tolerate incredible dullness .... There are such words as joy and sorrow, but they are only the burden of a psalm, sung with a nasal twang, while we believe in the ordinary and mean .... The life in us is like the water in the river. It may rise this year higher than man has ever known it, and flood the parched uplands; even this may be the eventful year ...." The new dawn is up to the individual himself, however; for "only that day dawns to which we are awake."

Comment

It is clear that the waters of life rose higher in Thoreau than ever before during his stay at Walden. There he discovered, through simplifying his life, the novelty of the world, and particularly the world of Nature. It can be said that he went farthest toward fashioning that perfect "staff" of his work and his life during this period of voluntary withdrawal from the outside world. The fable of the beautiful bug (with which he closes) that came out of the egg in the dry leaf of an old applewood table in one of hope, of organic renewal. "Who knows what beautiful and winged life, whose egg has been buried for ages under many concentric layers of woodenness in the dead dry life of society, deposited at first in the alburnum of the green and living tree, which has been gradually converted into the semblance of its well-seasoned tomb ... may unexpectedly come forth from amidst society's most trivial and handselled furniture, to enjoy its perfect summer life at last!" This is what the experience of Walden has meant to him, what he has attempted to describe in the symbolism of the deep pond (his inner self), the four seasons (the cycles of life, its stages), the thaw (re-awakening) and especially spring (purification and rebirth).

ON THE DUTY OF CIVIL DISOBEDIENCE

Thoreau begins this now-famous essay by agreeing with the motto, "That government is best which governs least." He explains: "For government is an expedient by which men would fain succeed in letting one another alone; and, as has been said, when it is most expedient, the governed are most let alone by it." He realizes, however, that this sort of government can come only when men "are prepared for it"; and he adds, "to speak practically and as a citizen, unlike those who call themselves no-government men, I ask for, not at once no government, but at once a better government."

Comment

The reader will recall the incident (mentioned in Chapter IV of *Walden*) of Thoreau's arrest in July, 1846, for refusal to pay his poll tax. Although somebody paid his tax for him, his night in jail was a gesture the theory behind which he importantly enlarges upon in this essay. His essential view was that government should further the social welfare; when it does not, the individual citizen has the right to resist.

There is to Thoreau (as to most of the Transcendentalists) a right of conscience which supersedes on urgent enough occasions the rights of law and government. And he asks, "can there not be a government in which majorities do not virtually decide right and wrong, but conscience? - in which majorities decide only those questions to which the rule of expediency is applicable?" What Thoreau pleads for is a kind of "wise minority" with the courage to assert itself in some perhaps passive yet effective manner against government which seems neglectful of the people's needs or whose actions are unwise. The specific issues for Thoreau were slavery, and the war in Mexico: "this people must cease to hold slaves, and to make war on Mexico," he asserts. As for passive effectiveness he says, "A minority is powerless when it conforms to the majority … but it is irresistible when it clogs by its whole weight. If the alternative is to keep all just men in prison, or give up war and slavery, the State will not hesitate which to choose." Thus "those who call themselves Abolitionists should at once effectually withdraw their support, both in person and property, from the government of Massachusetts, and not wait till they constitute a majority of one, before they suffer the right to prevail through them. I think that it is enough if they have God on their side, without waiting for that other one. Moreover, any man more right than his neighbors constitutes a majority of one already." [Thoreau became particularly devoted to the Abolitionist cause in later years.]

He then relates his own encounter with the American government in the person of the local tax collector, his "civil neighbor," whom he has obliged to consider his official representative position by refusing to pay his poll-tax and going to jail. He concedes, however, that when he discusses the current issues "with the freest of my neighbors, I perceive that, whatever they may say about the magnitude and seriousness of the question, and their regard for the public tranquillity, the long and the short of the matter is, that they cannot spare the protection of the existing government, and they dread the consequences to their property and families of disobedience to it." As for Thoreau, however, in the case of government which allows one sixth of the population to remain in slavery and permits its army to unjustly overrun a foreign country, he willingly incurs the penalty of civil disobedience rather than obey the laws of such a state. That he was imprisoned for not paying his poll-tax (in actuality he had not paid it for six years) is proof that "the State never intentionally confronts a man's sense, intellectual or moral, but only his body, his senses." Typically, Thoreau used his night in jail for close observation, conversing with a fellow-prisoner and detailing the strange place: the experience was "like travelling into a far country," and Thoreau was ever intent upon broadening his universe.

Thoreau is equally eager to point out, though, that one must constantly re-examine such acts of civil disobedience: "one cannot be too much on his guard in such a case, lest his action be biased by obstinacy or an undue regard for the opinions of men. Let him see that he does only what belongs to himself and to the hour." Thus he realizes that such actions must be more reasoned than spontaneous, more founded in theory than in impulse. He insists, "I do not wish to quarrel with any man or nation. I do not wish to split hairs, to make fine distinctions, or set myself up as better than my neighbors, I seek rather, I may say, even an excuse for conforming the laws of the land. I am but too ready to conform to them." He believes, however, that often "statesmen and legislators, standing so completely within the institution, never distinctly and nakedly behold it." He has admiring but mixed feeling about Daniel Webster, for example, who while he deserves to be called "the Defender of the Constitution," is yet "unable to take a fact out of its merely political relations, and behold it as it lies absolutely to be disposed of by the intellect- what, for instance, it behooves a man to do here in America today with regard to slavery ...." American legislators in general are, he suggests, too fond of oratory and eloquence for its own sake instead of truth for its own sake. He thus concludes that "the authority of government, even such as I am willing to submit to-for I will cheerfully obey those who know and can do better than I, and in many things even those who neither know nor can do so well-is still an impure one: to be strictly just, it must have the sanction and consent of the governed. It can have no pure right over my person and property but what I concede to it. The progress from an absolute to a limited monarchy, from a limited monarchy to a democracy, is a progress toward a true respect for the individual." To Thoreau, the "free and enlightened State" is one which will "recognize the individual as a higher and independent power, from which all its own power and authority are derived."

Comment

Thoreau is here at his lucid best, in thought and in style (proving his versatility, ranging from the poetic symbolism of his maturing philosophy to cogent, incisive comment and affirmation on the state of his own society). He will support his government so long as its ends are moral; when they are not, he must resist. Then he becomes part of the "wise minority" - which might be an enlightened individual - in urging that government to revise its policies in foreign affairs and at home, in the matter of highways, schools, conservation as well as in the major issue of slavery.

It is important to note that the civil disobedience outlined by Thoreau is not really so passive; in clogging the machinery of the state, it acts as counter-friction. It undermines existing law by invoking the higher standard of moral law or conscience.

Thoreau's statements here have of course had more far-reaching effect than he could have dreamed upon the occasion of his personal protest and one-night's imprisonment: his ideas can be found in the British Labor Movement, in Mahatma Gandhi's Satyagraha and the tenets by which he lived, and more than a hundred years later, in the philosophy which activates many civil rights organizations as they combat the present crisis of obtaining equal rights and opportunities for minorities.

SELECTED POEMS

WITHIN THE CIRCUIT OF THIS PLODDING LIFE

Despite the title, this is a poem about freedom; Thoreau describes various beautiful images in nature and the happiness he has obtained from contemplating them. In his own magical way, he makes the promise they offer him real, and not full of dreamy idealism. The poem is an argument that man is "by God's cheap economy made rich." Thoreau has given it subtle, strong form by eliminating almost all logical, rhetorical, or persuasive figures of speech. A world of images makes the poem's argument, showing in every particular that the poet has lived what he says. The poem is written in blank verse.

I MAKE YE AN OFFER

This is a seemingly crude little poem in which Thoreau offers a wry, New Englander's covenant: "I make ye an offer,/ Ye, gods, hear the scoffer,/ The scheme will not hurt you,/ If ye will find goodness, I will find virtue." Actually, the poem is masterfully written in a way that undercuts the seeming vanity of the offer. The real **theme** of it becomes man's vanity and irrepressible desire for freedom. Thoreau manages this mostly through the rhyming couplets. Each couplet conceals or reveals something fallible about the speaker, considering the high business he is about. For example, "And I swear by the rood,/ I'll be slave to no God" seems full of resolution for a moment, until we remember the poem is supposed to be addressed to "Gods" and that the rood is the cross - the oldest and most revered symbol of God. There is a different kind of human absurdity concealed in each **couplet**, until the last two lines spring the central meaning: "And give him a sphere/Somewhat larger than here." This says nothing too different from the other requests, but says it with such direct authority and dignity that we feel man may be better than the world he has been given, and deserves more freedom. It is only by living so fully in the natural world God had given him that Thoreau could achieve the uniquely intimate and commonsensical tone of this "offer" to God. The poem is in rhymed **couplets** and basically iambic **trimeter**. (For further explication of this poem see Question 5 in the Question and Answer section.)

OTHER POEMS

Like Emerson, Thoreau's notions about the art of poetry were not formalized in an essay. Like Emerson also, he found the basis of poetry in beauty, truth, and goodness. Not opposed to the **didactic**, he required that poetry be ethical as well as beautiful. "Friendship" is a good example of this. It is one of his best statements of the ideal standards he held for friendship. His demands were so exacting, so complete, that not one of the remarkable men or women he knew was able to fulfill them: "Implacable is Love,/ Foes may be bought or teased/ From their hostile intent, /But he goes unappeased/ Who is on kindness bent." "Nature Doth Have Her Dawn Each Day" expresses the young Thoreau's complete confidence in the teachings of Emerson. "Sic Vita," which starts, "I am a parcel of vain striving tied/ By a chance bond together," is one of Thoreau's earliest general statements about life. One can guess the serious tenor of life in the Transcendentalist community from the fact that Thoreau used it as a courtship poem to the one woman in his life. He threw it in her window with a bunch of violets loosely tied with straw. "Haze" and "Smoke" are two poems which display the mastery Thoreau achieved over the Greek poets. Emerson said they were better than their models.

PERSONALITY IN POETRY

Thoreau's reputation as a poet has climbed steadily since his own day. A recent critic has declared: "Thoreau, like Emily Dickinson ... anticipates the bold symbolism, airy impressionism, stringent **realism**, and restless inconsistencies of twentieth century poetry." In considering his verse, one must keep in mind Emerson's remark that Thoreau's biography was in his verses. That is to say, one must always remember that the authority for his poems is not any discreet independent voice of truth, but an essentially autobiographical truth. Word to word, image to image, his poems may change simply because he is the kind of man who would change that way. This creation and dramatization of personality is a great achievement in Thoreau. We hear a whole man behind his poems, body, soul, experience, every particle of being. This is an unmistakable sign of a master poet. Thoreau brought no particular method to verse - that is, no established method. He used what he could from the classics, from the seventeenth-century metaphysicals, from Chaucer, and Ben Jonson - and from Emerson. The stage of *Walden* is so firmly set in our minds that it is hard to see how completely Thoreau created himself in his poetry. One imagines one has been told in prose what is actually there of his personality in verse.

Comment

Thoreau's conduct was supremely logical. He applied, in his everyday rambles through the fields, the same principles that his neighbors assented to on the Sabbath. The more one thinks of him, the more honest, fearless and inquisitive Thoreau seems - and the more strange the practical Yankees around him seem. He despised exploiting himself or his fellow man because he concluded that "the cost of a thing is the amount of what I will call life which is required to be exchanged for it, immediately or in the long run." The cost of his poetry was great. Every complexity of it, every oddness and indirection was aimed at finding a way he could more fully live-nothing in it seems a merely formal or conventional poetical resolution. Thoreau was a poet enough to want very deeply to pay the cost of his poetry. He wanted it to be as alive as he was.

CRITICAL COMMENTARY

As is true of most writers who have offered any sort of controversial material to the world, Thoreau, along with his most representative writings *Walden* and "On the Duty of Civil Disobedience," has met with a fluctuating critical appraisal over the years. In general, however, his own contemporaries emphasized the doctrine of simplicity and the inherent romanticism in a work like *Walden*, ignoring or misunderstanding its deeper philosophy and symbolism; these same readers likewise dismissed the essay on civil disobedience as eccentric. On the other hand, in modern times there has been a not unnatural re-evaluation of Thoreau (for all major American writers have been re-examined in the light of 20th century criticism) tending in the opposite direction of his complexities of thought.

THOREAU THE MAN

We might begin with the image of Thoreau as one of those "young men of fairest promise" whom Emerson addressed in "The American Scholar" as they were graduating from Harvard in 1837. On this commencement occasion Emerson described such men, "who begin life upon our shores, inflated by the mountain winds, shined upon by all the stars of God," yet who "find the earth below not in unison with these," since they "are hindered from action by the disgust which the principles on which business is managed inspire ..." Apparently Thoreau took such words strictly to heart; he became, as Oliver Wendell Holmes later observed in what was the judgment of his own generation, a "nullifier of civilization." His biographers, such as Henry Seidel Canby and Carl Bode, tend to see him as essentially introverted; Canby, for example (Thoreau, 1939), calls him a "dreamy child," one who "hated games, street parades and shows .... company in the house," and "loved nature more than man," Even his contemporary and friend Emerson, in his famous "Biographical Sketch," commented: "There was somewhat military in his nature not to be subdued, always manly and able, but rarely tender, as if he did not feel himself except in opposition. He ... required a little sense of victory."

COMPLEXITY OF WALDEN

It may be too that Thoreau's biographies infer a good deal from his major work, *Walden*, whose stylistic method and content seem to have been misunderstood by his earliest readers and critics, an evaluation that to some extent has followed the writing down to the present. His symbolism, for instance, they considered extravagant "namby-pamby" or "stuff," and chose to read *Walden* in terms of its simplified, direct style. As for the content, these readers concentrated upon Thoreau's act of withdrawal from society (just as they concentrated upon his distaste for authority in "On the Duty of Civil Disobedience") and at best, read the book as social gospel which entreated the individual to escape from corrupting civilization into the woods. These readers thus emphasized the romantic, escapist, back-to-Nature aspects of *Walden* at the expense of the larger philosophical, symbolic implications of the work. Modern critics however admit *Walden*'s full complexity, granting it all the above-mentioned elements and more. They view it, for example, as a major work of social criticism of its time, in which Thoreau certainly was proclaiming against the stultifying influence of his American society upon the souls of men: these critics credit Thoreau with analyzing these degrading influences upon mankind, with suggesting alternatives or solutions through his educational, cultural and political theories, with strongly urging the substitution of selfhood - the search for the soul or inner nature - for racing after material wealth and power. As one Thoreau expert points out (Sherman Paul in his edition of *Walden*, 1957), "to get men to see their universe symbolically, to read beyond its lessons of matter-of-fact, was one of the most liberating things Thoreau had to offer." "Not an escape, but the greatest discovery and gift," Paul goes on to say, was what Thoreau offered through the experience of Walden. In other words, Thoreau was trying to persuade us to re-examine our lives, to become more aware of our inner selves. Walden, then, which combines the record of Thoreau's experiment of living two years in the woods with his reflective view of this experience in the years afterward (from 1847 to 1854), relates essentially the author's personal struggle for purity, union with Nature and selfhood in the midst of his own practical existence- in other words, Thoreau's spiritual autobiography.

THOREAU'S CONTEMPORARIES

We can examine briefly, however what some of Thoreau's contemporaries thought about *Walden* and its author, and what the present-day view is, including some cases of special- pleading (such as that of E. B. White, whose involvement with Thoreau has been a long one). There are two rather well-known comments, for example, by near-contemporaries: James Russell

Lowell and Robert Louis Stevenson. Lowell, of course, seems to have been very different in personality and moral outlook from Thoreau, yet his review of Thoreau's Letters to Various Persons, with general commentary. (*North American Review*, 1865) proved influential. Remarking (in the editorial "we") that he has currently been recollecting Thoreau's writings, Lowell attempts to give his impressions: "He seems to us to have been a man with so high a conceit of himself that he accepted without questioning, and insisted on our accepting, his defects and weaknesses of character as virtues and powers peculiar to himself. Was he [if he is] indolent, he finds none of the activities which attract or employ the rest of mankind worthy of him. Was he wanting in the qualities that make success, it is success that is contemptible, and not himself that lacks persistency and purpose. Was he poor, money was an unmixed evil." Lowell, in short, sees Thoreau as a prime rationalizer, further borne out in the remark, "It is curious, considering what Thoreau afterwards became, that he was not by nature an observer. He only saw the things he looked for, and was less poet than naturalist." Stevenson (*Cornhill Magazine*, 1880) makes more of an objective attempt to assess Thoreau, beginning with the assertion that "Thoreau's art was literature; and it was one of which he had conceived most ambitiously." He then discusses that "art," adding that "Thoreau's true subject was the pursuit of self-improvement combined with an unfriendly criticism of life as it goes on in our societies; it is there that he best displays the freshness and surprising trenchancy of his intellect; it is there that his style becomes plain and vigorous, and therefore, according to his own formula, ornamental." One of the most favorable comments on Thoreau, however, comes in an anonymous contemporary review from the National Anti-Slavery Standard of December 16, 1854 (reprinted in Walter Harding's *Thoreau: A Century of Criticism*, 1954-Harding calls this review "unquestionably the best criticism of Thoreau's writings that appeared in his lifetime"). It is worth quoting at some length, since it captures the spirit of Thoreau's intent.

These books [*A Week* and *Walden*] spring from a depth of thought which will not suffer them to be put by, and are written in a spirit in striking contrast with that which is uppermost in our time and country. Out of the heart of practical, hard-working, progressive New England come these Oriental utterances. The life exhibited in them teaches us, much more impressively than any number of sermons could, that this Western activity of which we are so proud, these material improvements, this commercial enterprise, this rapid accumulation of wealth, even our external, associated philanthropic action, are very easily overrated ... It is refreshing to find in these books the sentiments of one man whose aim manifestly is to live, and not to waste his time upon the externals of living. Educated at Cambridge [Harvard], in the way called liberal, he seems determined to make a liberal life of it, and not to become the slave of any calling, for the sake of earning a reputable livelihood or of being regarded as a useful member of society. He evidently considers it his first business to become more and more a living, advancing soul, knowing that thus alone ... can he be, in any proper sense, useful to others ... The fact of surpassing interest for us is the simple grandeur of Mr. Thoreau's position-a position open to us all, and of which this sympathy with Nature is but a single result.

PRACTICAL VS. IMPRACTICAL

One approach to modern criticism of Thoreau is from the angle of controversy over the practical vs. the impractical Thoreau, represented by at least two contemporary critics, Louis B. Salomon and Wade Thompson (in essays appearing in *College English*, 1956-1957). Mr. Salomon evokes a "practical Thoreau" to counter eight objections which he suggests students invariably bring up in their studies of Thoreau; it is Mr. Thompson's task to prove that these very objections raised by students are actually rather sound, given Thoreau's expressed opinions-his conclusion is that Thoreau is certainly inconsistent and that he is (as Robert Louis Stevenson also suggested) an exaggerator. To conclude thus, however, according to Thompson, is not necessarily to be bound to dismiss Thoreau. The objections to Thoreau are already familiar: 1) Thoreau thought he was better than anybody else; 2) Thoreau didn't recognize the benefits of commerce and machinery; 3) Thoreau was completely opposed to organized society and government; 4) Thoreau thought people shouldn't do any work; 5) Thoreau thought all material comforts were bad influences; 6) Thoreau didn't recognize the practical side of life; 7) Thoreau was a hermit; 8) Thoreau is trying to tell us how we should arrange our lives. In the case of each "student" objection, which Salomon has answered with refuting quotations from *Walden* and "Civil Disobedience," Thompson counters further with quotations which sustain the student objections! For example, that Thoreau "didn't recognize the benefits of commerce and machinery" is answered by Salomon with "I have always endeavored to acquire strict business habits; they are indispensable to every man." Thompson reminds the reader of Thoreau's summarial statement, "Trade curses everything it handles; and though you trade in messages from Heaven, the whole curse of trade attaches to the business." Or take the matter of material comforts as "bad influences": Salomon quotes, "My greatest skill has been to want but little. A lady once offered me a mat, but as I had no room to spare within the house, nor time to spare within or without to shake it, I declined it, preferring to wipe my feet on the sod before my door. It is best to avoid the beginning of evil." As Thompson ironically observes, "When a door-mat is evil, material comforts look pretty bad." As for his own countering quotation from *Walden*, Thompson cites, "I believe that water is the only drink for a wise man; wine is not so noble a liquor; and think of dashing the hopes of a morning with a cup of warm coffee, or of an evening with a dish of tea! ... Such apparently slight causes destroyed Greece and Rome, and will destroy England and America." As a matter of fact, both of the passages cited emphasize Thoreau's "exaggerated" asceticism. Such refutations and counter-refutations perhaps focus upon the danger (and possibly inherent hilarity) of trying to find consistent ideology in poet philosophers. Indeed, this is Wade Thompson's conclusion; "My main point is that Thoreau, on a literal residual level, is virtually amorphous. He is practical or impractical, prophet or blind man, naturalist or supernaturalist, 'a clammy prig' or a warm genial companion-depending almost totally on how one chooses to look at him. That students reject him for being impractical is-I hope I have demonstrated-only too understandable. In this respect I disagree with Mr. Salomon, who says: 'I hate to hear them [students] waste time arguing against him for things he not only didn't say but repeatedly and explicitly disavowed.' They are 'tilting at windmills that aren't even there.' The windmills are there all right; they are there in abundance-disavowals or no. These very windmills have been tilted at by men like Emerson and Stevenson and Lowell ..."

CONTEMPORARY VIEWS

Two contemporary examples of "special pleading" - at least, of special points of view-are of interest: one draws a modern analogy to Thoreau's *Walden* and his philosophy; the other calls him "Christian in spite of himself." Wright Morris ("To the Woods," in *The Territory Ahead*, 1958) suggests that Thoreau shaped the natural grain of the Yankee mind in a way which is still applicable, with his concept of Nature. Morris pinpoints the issue of his article with an ironic and incisive quotation from D.

H. Lawrence, another eminent commentator on American life and letters:

Nature

I wish I could write it larger than that.

Nature

Benjamin [Franklin] overlooked Nature. But the French Crevecoeur spotted it long before Thoreau and Emerson worked it up. Absolutely the safest thing to get your emotional reactions over is Nature.

The problem then and now, according to Morris, is *Nature vs. Human Nature*; and he believes that "somewhere between Walden Pond and Boston-at some point of tension ... the schizoid soul of the American is polarized. On the one hand we are builders of bridges and cities, we are makers of things and believers in the future. On the other we have a powerful, private urge to take to the woods, as we so often do." As further evidence of analogy between the time of Walden and now, as regards the problem of human existence, Morris quotes Thoreau thus: "I should not talk about myself so much if there were anybody else whom I knew as well. Unfortunately I am confined to this by the narrowness of my experience." This is Morris' conclusion: "The revelation of this statement may lead us to overlook its accuracy. The narrowness of his experience is one of the essential facts in his book. I am not concerned with the absence of those things that we now exploit. On such matters as woman and sex we can respect his silence. What he chooses to tell us is much more to the point ... I would like to suggest that the myth of Nature-writ large, as Thoreau wrote it-can be as overwhelming, traumatic in fact, as the myth of Sex. It is the myth of Nature that concerns us in Thoreau. He turned to Nature as D. H. Lawrence turned to Sex, and both transformed what they saw, what they found, to suit the needs of their genius and their temperament. It is difficult to say which offers the greater handicap. Each man sees, in the mirror of his choice, what he is compelled to see. For all of the material details, the counting of nails and beans, Walden Pond is a mythic, personal vision, and in its depths lurk such facts as it is the genius of the beholder to see."

THOREAU AND RELIGION

Michael F. Moloney is concerned with Thoreau's "Christianity" (in "Christian *Malgré Lui*," *American Classics Reconsidered*, 1958). Because of Thoreau's avowed pantheism (which sees Nature as imbued with God) and his acquired, somewhat superficial orientalism overlaid on his inherited Puritanism, Walden is regarded as a search for spiritual certainty. To Mr. Moloney this is a wrong emphasis, for Thoreau was still involved in a form of Christianity and Christian principles. He observes summarily that "Thoreau's passion for nature, his reaction against the growing materialism of his day, his deep-seated ethical, and less deep-seated but no less genuine, religious concerns - these are the materials upon whose intractability his creative imagination and his magnificent gift for phrase sought to impose a final form." He admits that "the problem of Thoreau's religion does not admit of easy solution. He early 'signed off' from the Christianity of his youth. He did not go to church. At times he writes with what seems calculated irreverence." Yet the writer believes that "Thoreau's negations, far from revealing an unsympathetic attitude, are better considered as a clearing of ground for his statement of affirmatives. No careful reader will doubt that he was a reverent man." In fact, "at a time when Yankee ingenuity was subduing the earth, and the gospel of success was proclaimed from every street corner and town hall, he came to preach an older and more abstemious doctrine. Intuitively, he seems to have experienced the conviction that behind the Puritan virtues of thrift and industry and provident concern with material things lay the rather more than half-neglected truths which gave these things meaning-truths which Puritanism itself, in its best moments, remembered. In an age which was rapidly reducing all values to one value and all standards to one standard, and these not of the highest, he set himself in the name of humanity against the tide. Walden, which describes his relationship with his epoch is, ultimately a humanist manifesto... Man is Thoreau's primary concern, not God. However, he was still near enough to the Christianity which he outwardly rejected to be quite certain that man without the Spirit is not man." To this writer, then, Walden becomes a Christian humanist document.

THE CRITIC E. B. WHITE

It is perhaps fitting to close this commentary with remarks of one writer - E. B. White - who has known Walden for years (since 1927), recognizes the virtues, the vices, the eccentricities of Thoreau, and writes delightfully about it all. What he has written in several essays tends to bring together issues and answer questions which have been raised above. White observes, for example (*The New Yorker*, 1949), that "Thoreau has probably been more wildly misconstrued than any other person of comparable literary stature. He got a reputation for being a naturalist, and he was not much of a naturalist. He got a reputation for being a hermit, and he was no hermit. He was a writer, is what he was. Many regarded him as a poseur. He was a poseur, all right, but the pose was struck not for other people to study but for him to study-a brave and ingenious device for a creative person to adopt. He posed for himself and was both artist and model, examining his own position in relation to nature and society with the most patient and appreciative care … Henry was torn all his days between two awful pulls - the gnawing desire to change life, and the equally troublesome desire to live it. This is the explanation of his excursion." As White goes on to say, what seemed "so wrong to him was less man's economy than man's puny spirit and man's strained relationship with nature" - that is, Thoreau was not strictly a social reformer. White observes, though, that to admire Walden today "is something of an embarrassment, for the mass of men have an indistinct notion that its author was a sort of Nature Boy." Thus he raises and answers the question of Thoreau's devotion to Nature. "If Thoreau had merely left us an account of a man's life in the woods, or if he had simply retreated to the woods and there recorded his complaints about society, or even if he had contrived to include both records in one essay, 'Walden' would probably not have lived a hundred years …. Thoreau, very likely without knowing quite what he was up to, took man's relation to nature and man's dilemma in society and man's capacity for elevating his spirit and he beat all these matters together, in a wild free interval of self justification and delight …. 'Walden' is one of the first of the vitamin-enriched American dishes." White certainly considers it unfair to assess Thoreau's stay at the pond as escapism; "to set it down to escapism is, of course, to misconstrue what happened. Henry went forth to battle when he took to the woods, and 'Walden' is the report of a man torn by two powerful and opposing drives - the desire to enjoy the world … and the urge to set the world straight. One cannot join these two successfully, but sometimes, in rare cases, something good or even great results from the attempt of the tormented spirit to reconcile them." White concludes that Thoreau "was the subtlest humorist of the nineteenth century, a most religious man, and was awake every moment."

It can be said of *Walden*, then (and of Thoreau's thought in general), that like in many classic works (the Old English *Beowulf*, Chaucer's *Canterbury Tales*, Swift's *Gulliver's Travels*, Voltaire's *Candide*, Hemingway's short stories), it clothes in deceptive simplicity (including style) its literary worth and philosophic depth.

ESSAY QUESTIONS AND ANSWERS

....

Question: Describe briefly Thoreau's concept of Nature as seen in *Walden*.

Answer: Thoreau's view of Nature is essentially the American Transcendentalist view also, that a) it is a benevolent force; b) that it is to be enjoyed and reverenced; c) through Nature there is not only knowledge from the five senses but also intuitive knowledge; d) the ultimate goal is a feeling of communion, unity with Nature. For Thoreau the most direct line of communication was between the self and Nature. With this goal in view he developed his doctrine of simplicity - that is, he "went to the woods in order to live deliberately, to front only the essentials of life." In Nature, consequently, a man is nearest to God and godlikeness. He also felt it imperative to observe Nature's phenomena carefully, since there was a "correspondence" between every fact of Nature and the consciousness of man. Ideally, every physical fact of Nature could be absorbed into the mind; complete absorption resulted in the feeling of oneness with Nature, as well as a sense of liberation which, hopefully, could be passed on to one's fellow man.

Question: What is Thoreau's view of "civilized" society?

Answer: To Thoreau, civilized society is really a "barbarizing" element. In other words, the goals which the majority of civilized men subscribe to - material success, the work ethic, organized authority, general "busy-ness" - are barbarizing in the sense that they obscure from them their inner nature, that higher self to be searched for and found at the center of each man. Thoreau, for example, all his life detested the necessity for making a living, contending that it made his life "coarse." When first out of college, he resisted the pressures to join, as a Harvard graduate, the ranks of clergymen or lawyers or academics - he chose, at last, to wander as poet-philosopher, never really fulfilling the standards of the society of Massachusetts (and the whole America) around him.

Also, he considered his particular society - America - and his own state - Massachusetts - barbaric and brutal in the sense that its government permitted - thus condoned - slavery, and in foreign affairs, "overran unjustly" the territory of other countries such as Mexico. His position was that the individual, as part of a "wise minority" which might consist of just himself, had the right of conscience to challenge such government. He spoke and wrote essays on this subject.

Question: List a few details of Thoreau's actual life at Walden Pond, especially those which illustrate his "doctrine of simplicity."

Answer: In *Walden* Thoreau describes the test of "inner necessities" of a man which he seems to have applied both in fact and in theory; that is, he details the very physical environment he constructed for himself during the two years at Walden and at the same time, he suggests, in parallel manner, what are and are not the necessities of mankind with respect to food, clothing, shelter. Thoreau lived as a vegetarian, for example; he did not even care for the fish he caught in Walden Pond, preferring the "cleaner potatoes he might cook, and bread he might make for himself. Likewise, he dressed simply and functionally, and he observes how unfunctional much of man's costume is; rather, he says, it is designed to conform to the current fashion, which often has little eye for comfort or utility. As for shelter, he contended that our houses are in general too big, too wasteful and too uncomfortable, as well as just plain ugly. His ideal for shelter was realized in the modest one-room hut he constructed by himself (except for a few week's help from a friend on the masonry), a house that was flexible with the seasons: in the summer he left it unplastered and open, so that the clean, fresh air passed through daily and he could feel the impact of mornings; in the winter, although insulated with plaster and a fireplace and shingles, he lived simply, cooking on his open fireplace (the first year - the second brought a cook stove which he found "unpoetic"). And his own daily schedule was flexible according to the seasons, too, but essentially was comprised of fulfilling the necessities such as procuring food, water and firewood, reading and meditating in the morning and often the evening hours, walking in the woods and observing Nature, sometimes visiting friends in the village.

Question: Describe briefly the use of symbolism and **imagery** in *Walden*.

Answer: The basic symbolism of *Walden* is of the seasons and of the pond; within these are the day, the dawn, the spring, the thaw, the reptilian **imagery**. Although the stay at Walden encompassed two years, in Walden (experienced in 1846-7 but published in 1854) he has condensed this time into one year and the four seasons which roughly parallel seasons of the mind and heart.

(Winter, for instance, is a time of partial isolation from Nature, and of meditation, and somewhat, of discontent.) Spring figures largely and exuberantly in the scheme, symbolizing purification and rebirth; here, and in other chapters, he signifies the blessed change from an old life to a fresher new life by the shedding of skin, by reptilian **imagery**. The thaw, too, is symbolic of this shedding of old life; and the entire phenomenon of the thaw was an exhilarating experience to Thoreau. The day also has its seasons like the year, and its essential one is dawn or morning, when, according to Thoreau, the mind is most alert: "only that day dawns," he asserts, "to which we are fully awake."

Question: Briefly describe the background of Thoreau's essay, "On the Duty of Civil Disobedience."

Answer: Technically, this essay is based on the incident of Thoreau's refusal to pay poll tax, and his arrest and imprisonment in July of 1846. He had, however, refused to pay such tax since 1842, and did refuse after the incident (but as in 1846, friends paid the tax for him); for his motives went deeper than this mere omission. He had lectured and written on the nature of civil disobedience before issuing this illustrative essay in 1849. The greatest specific objection Thoreau had to his government (of Massachusetts, and his own state as representative of the nation) was its brutal condoning of slavery within its bounds (and in later life Thoreau became an ardent Abolitionist); secondarily, he objected to America's going to war in Mexico. Spending only one night in jail actually deprived him of testing the tax - and thus of challenging the government - in short deprived him of desirable publicity as the objecting individual citizen: so he wrote the essay.

Question: According to Thoreau, what does civil disobedience mean?

Answer: The enlightened individual citizen-one who is thoughtful and aware-has a right of conscience, says Thoreau, which supersedes the laws of governments. This is moral law (which the Transcendentalists believed supreme). The individual, then, has responsibility to challenge his government when and where he thinks it is wrong. His action is defined as passive resistance, but it is hardly so passive as it seems, since it is designed to throw cogs in the machinery of government (Thoreau's gesture of refusing to pay the tax is comparable to Gandhi's fasting, or to present-day sit-ins, teach-ins, demonstrations and marches in behalf of civil rights causes in America). He insists at the same time that he-like any enlightened individual citizen-is only too ready to support the government when it furthers the social welfare-in the issues (current to him) of slavery and wars abroad, and in education, culture, transportation, reform.

BIBLIOGRAPHY AND GUIDE TO RESEARCH PAPERS

....

Burroughs, John. "Thoreau's Wildness," *Critic*, I (1881), 74-75. Reprinted in Harding, *A Century of Criticism*.

Canby, Henry Seidel. *Thoreau*. Boston, 1939. A perceptive biography. Out in paperback.

Christy, Arthur. *The Orient in American Transcendentalism*. New York, 1932. Studies the influence of Eastern philosophy on Thoreau and others.

Feidelson, Charles. *Symbolism and American Literature*. Chicago, 1953.

Harding, Walter, ed. *Thoreau: A Century of Criticism*. Dallas, 1954. Contains many interesting articles, including the anonymous review cited herein.

Harding, Thomas. *A Thoreau Handbook*. New York, 1959.

Hicks, John H. ed. "Thoreau: A Centenary Gathering," *Minnesota Review*, IV (1962), 41-172. Many contributors who have written in the past on Thoreau.

Holmes, Oliver Wendell. *Ralph Waldo Emerson*. Boston, 1893. Contains comments on Thoreau.

Hyman, Stanley Edgar. "Henry Thoreau in Our Time." *Atlantic Monthly* (November, 1946), 137-146.

Krutch, Joseph Wood. *Henry David Thoreau.* New York, 1948. Not only biography but study of Thoreau's ideas and art.

Leary, Lewis. "A Century of Walden," *Nation*, CXXXVI (1933), 506-507.

Lowell, James Russell. "Thoreau," in *My Study Windows.* Boston, 1871.

Matthiessen, F. O. *American Renaissance.* New York, 1941. Essay on Thoreau's ideas in connection with other Transcendentalists.

Meitzer, Milton, and Walter Harding. *A Thoreau Profile.* New York, 1962. A biography which utilizes passages by Thoreau and his contemporaries.

Miller, Perry. "One Night in the Concord Jail," *The Reporter,* 23 January 1958, 48.

Moloney, Michael F. "Christian *Malgré Lui,"* in *American Classics Reconsidered*, ed. Harold C. Gardiner. New York, 1958.

Morris, Wright. *The Territory Ahead.* New York, 1958.

Paul, Sherman, ed. *Collected Critical Essays.* New York, 1962. In paperback.

_____. *The Shores of America: Thoreau's Inward Exploration.* Urbana, 1958.

_____. Edition of *Walden*, with long introduction and other material of interest.

Salomon, Louis B. "The Practical Thoreau," *College English*, XVII (1956), 229-232. See Thompson's article.

Salt, H. S. *The Life of Henry David Thoreau.* London, 1896. A fairly balanced early biography.

Seybold, Ethel. *Thoreau: The Quest and the Classics.* New Haven, 1951. Study of Thoreau as student of the Greek and Roman classics.

Shanley, James L. *The Making of Walden.* Chicago, 1947. Text of the first version, with explanation.

Stevenson, Robert Louis. *Familiar Studies of Men and Books.* London, 1886.

Thompson, Wade. "The Impractical Thoreau," *College English*, XIX (1957-8), 67-70.

Thoreau, Henry David. *Collected Poems of Henry Thoreau,* ed. Carl Bode. Chicago, 1943. Treats his early career and production.

_____. *The Correspondence of Henry David Thoreau*, ed. Walter Harding and Carl Bode. Contains all available letters to and from Thoreau.

_____. *Walden, Civil Disobedience*, ed. Sherman Paul. Boston, 1957. In paperback.

Van Doren, Mark. *Henry David Thoreau: A Critical Study.* Boston, 1916. An important study dealing with Thoreau's ideas alone.

Walcutt, Charles C. "Thoreau in the Twentieth Century," *South Atlantic Quarterly*, XXXIX (1940), 168-184.

Whicher, George F. *Walden Revisited.* Chicago, 1945.

White, E. B. "Henry Thoreau," *The New Yorker*, 7 May 1949, 23.

_____. "The Retort Transcendental," *The Second Tree from the Corner.* New York, 1953.

_____. "Walden 1954," *The Yale Review.* Autumn (1954), 13-22.

www.ingramcontent.com/pod-product-compliance
Lightning Source LLC
LaVergne TN
LVHW011736060526
838200LV00051B/3186